Corporate Director's Guidebook

EIGHTH EDITION

Corporate Laws Committee

AMERICAN BAR ASSOCIATION
Business Law Section

Cover design by Catherine Zaccarine.

Printed in the United States of America.

28 27 26 25 24   5 4 3 2 1

ISBN: 978-1-63905-546-3

Table of Contents

Foreword

This is the Eighth Edition of the *Corporate Director's Guidebook*. Since its initial publication in 1978, countless directors, business executives, advisors, students of corporate governance, and others have come to rely on the advice and commentary in the *Guidebook*.

The primary purpose of the *Guidebook* is to provide concise, practical guidance to corporate directors in meeting their responsibilities. The *Guidebook* focuses on the role of the individual director in the context of the duties and functions of the board and its key committees (audit, compensation, and nominating and governance). Although many director decisions and tasks occur against a legal backdrop, the *Guidebook* attempts to avoid legalisms.

Director decisions and oversight responsibilities are subject to a significant level of public and shareholder scrutiny. To help directors engage in effective oversight and decision-making processes in the current environment, the Eighth Edition emphasizes the following key topics:

- the role of directors in the engagement between a corporation and its shareholders;
- board composition, refreshment, diversity, skills, and compensation;
- executive compensation design, particularly as it relates to performance and risk;
- risk management, including processes for identification, assessment, and mitigation;
- crisis preparedness; and
- fiduciary duties with respect to mergers and acquisitions and defensive actions.

The *Guidebook* provides important information for directors of public companies and also is relevant to directors of all companies in understanding their duties and obligations. The Corporate Laws Committee hopes directors and their advisors will benefit from this Eighth Edition of the *Guidebook.*

Respectfully submitted,

Steven M. Haas
Chair, Corporate Laws Committee

Beth Berg
Igor Kirman
Co-Chairs, *Corporate Director's Guidebook* Task Force

Corporate Laws Committee

The Corporate Laws Committee of the Section of Business Law of the American Bar Association is composed of active or former practicing lawyers, law professors, regulators, and judges with corporate expertise. In addition to the *Corporate Director's Guidebook* and other scholarly writings, the Committee is responsible for the development of the *Model Business Corporation Act* (the *Model Act*).

The *Model Act*, first issued in 1950, has been adopted substantially in its entirety by 34 states, the District of Columbia, and Guam. In addition, important provisions have been adopted by many other states. The *Model Act* has played an important role in the development of corporate law in the United States and elsewhere.

The Committee serves as the standing editorial board for the *Model Act*, reviewing, revising, and updating its provisions on a continuing basis. Moreover, the Committee publishes the *Model Business Corporation Act Annotated*, a comprehensive compilation of the *Model Act* with cases and authorities relevant to its provisions.

The roster of active Committee participants during the publication of the Eighth Edition of the *Guidebook* (including appointed members, senior advisors, reporters, secretaries, consultants, and liaisons from other ABA committees) is listed below.

Claudia H. Allen
Chicago, IL

Beth E. Berg
Chicago, IL

Willard L. Boyd, III
Des Moines, IA

C. Kent Carlson
Seattle, WA

Mary Ann Carlson
Bratenahl, OH

Nathaniel L. Doliner
Tampa, FL

Michelle Adams Earley
Austin, TX

Karl John Ege
Seattle, WA

Patricia Enerio
Wilmington, DE

Professor Jessica Erickson
Richmond, VA

Andrea M. Farley
Atlanta, GA

Margaret M. Foran
Newark, NJ

Mary A. Francis
San Ramon, CA

Mark J. Gentile
Wilmington, DE

Maureen Brennan Gershanik
New Orleans, LA

Keir Gumbs
Washington, DC

Steven M. Haas
Richmond, VA

James J. Hanks, Jr.
Baltimore, MD

Carol Hansell
Toronto, ON

Keith F. Higgins
Boston, MA

James D. Honaker
Wilmington, DE

Michael Hutchings
Seattle, WA

Michele D. Johnson
Orange County, CA

William D. Johnston
Wilmington, DE

Igor Kirman
New York, NY

John H. Lawrence, Jr.
Hartford, CT

Professor Jonathan C. Lipson
Philadelphia, PA

Jill Louis
Dallas, TX

David B.H. Martin
Washington, DC

David C. McBride
Wilmington, DE

Sue Meng
New York, NY

John F. Olson
Washington, DC

Sarah Payne
Palo Alto, CA

Professor Elizabeth Pollman
Philadelphia, PA

Professor Hillary A. Sale
Washington, DC

Philip Schwartz
Fort Lauderdale, FL

Larry P. Scriggins
Great Cacapon, WV

John A. Seethoff
Redmond, WA

The Honorable Collins J. Seitz, Jr.
Wilmington, DE

Professor Megan Wischmeier Shaner
Norman, OK

The Honorable Joseph R. Slights III
Wilmington, DE

Laurie A. Smiley
New Orleans, LA

A. Gilchrist Sparks, III
Wilmington, DE

Professor Robert B. Thompson
Washington, DC

The Honorable E. Norman Veasey
Wilmington, DE

Glenn D. West
Dallas, TX

R. Daniel Witschey, Jr.
Houston, TX

John Mark Zeberkiewicz
Wilmington, DE

Part I:
Preliminary Matters

CHAPTER

1 Overview

This edition of the *Corporate Director's Guidebook*, like its predecessors, focuses on director rights and duties as well as the allocation of rights and duties among directors, shareholders, and management. Shareholders elect directors but do not manage the corporation. The primary objective of the *Guidebook* is to provide practical guidance to those who are considering serving as directors and to those who are already serving as directors. The *Guidebook* covers key topics, including:

- what a person should consider before joining a board;
- director duties (including in special situations and under the federal securities laws);
- the role of the board with respect to risk oversight and compliance;
- how boards and board committees are structured and operate;
- the role and operations of the audit, compensation, and nominating and governance committees;
- the relationship between the board and shareholders; and
- protections for directors.

Although the *Guidebook* is primarily geared to public company directors, the *Guidebook* is relevant to all corporate directors. It provides a guide for the role of the board, as well as the functions, structure, and responsibilities of the board and its committees. The goal is to help directors effectively fulfill their duties to the corporation.

Today, most public company directors are independent directors (i.e., directors who are not employees of the corporation and are not directly involved in its daily operations). A key challenge for independent directors is to direct and oversee management of the corporation's activities and strategy in a dynamic environment using effective processes to make informed decisions and provide effective oversight, without becoming day-to-day managers. Like all directors, in doing so, these directors must be cognizant of their obligation to act free of conflicts and in what they perceive to be the best interests of the corporation. In determining the corporation's "best interests," directors should have in mind the interests of the shareholders as a whole. The *Guidebook* is designed to help directors meet that responsibility by explaining how they can best exercise their oversight and decision-making responsibilities through boardroom practices and procedures that promote effective director involvement.

U.S. public companies operate under a legal and regulatory framework that includes state law, federal law, the listing standards of the applicable securities exchanges, and laws outside the United States. With respect to matters of internal affairs, corporations are governed by the laws of the state in which they are incorporated. For corporate directors and the corporation itself, that means that the statutes and state court decisions of the state of incorporation will govern many corporate decisions and processes. As most large public companies are incorporated in Delaware, the *Guidebook* is primarily focused on the legal regime in Delaware, although it will also occasionally mention other jurisdictions and will touch on other types of regulations, such as U.S. federal securities laws. Public companies are also subject to federal securities laws and regulations and the listing standards of the major national securities exchanges; in this book, we refer to the two largest such exchanges, Nasdaq and the New York Stock Exchange, as the "U.S. stock exchanges."

The *Guidebook* addresses the federal securities law regime and, in general terms, the listing standards of the U.S. stock exchanges that mandate specific governance processes. The *Guidebook* does not, however, address industry-specific or other federal or state regulatory regimes, such as regulations that are uniquely applicable to financial institutions or utilities or anti-competition regulation. The *Guidebook* also does not address regulatory regimes outside the United States.

Readers should note that the *Guidebook* generally does not address controlled companies (i.e., companies of which a single person, entity, or group holds more than 50% of the voting power for the election of directors) or where there is a controlling shareholder. Special rules apply to controlled companies and, in certain circumstances, where there is a controlling shareholder. Directors of controlled companies and of corporations where there is a controlling shareholder should seek guidance from counsel regarding the particular rules, rights, and obligations that apply.

Most directors are not corporate lawyers. As a result, when appropriate, they should seek legal advice to ensure they satisfy legal requirements and properly support the board's deliberative decision-making processes. Although not all corporations have an internal general counsel, the *Guidebook* uses the term "general counsel" to refer to both internal and external lawyers who fulfill that role.

We hope the *Guidebook* is helpful to directors in understanding their duties and the role of the board as they undertake their important responsibilities.

CHAPTER

2 Joining a Board of Directors

There is no single process by which directors are selected and agree to sit on boards. Whether initially identified by a search firm, other directors, senior management, shareholders, or otherwise, director candidates typically engage in an iterative conversation with incumbent members of the board, sometimes while the board is engaged in parallel conversations with other potential candidates. A decision to join a board ultimately comes down to whether the candidate's experience, knowledge, skill set, and independent business judgment are a good strategic and cultural fit for the corporation and the board.

A. YOUR EVALUATION OF THE CORPORATION

As a candidate, you should perform your own independent diligence on the corporation and consider any information the corporation—or, if engaged, a professional search firm—may provide. Sources of information can include the corporation's website, filings with the Securities and Exchange Commission (SEC), press releases, news stories, analyst reports, and conversations with management representatives. Candidates usually meet with some combination of the chair of the board or the lead independent director, the chair of the nominating and governance committee, and the chief executive officer (CEO). Candidates may also meet with other members of the nominating and governance committee or the full board. These conversations should provide insight into the corporation's strategic goals and challenges, its business, history, culture, competitive environment, financial condition (including recent changes), potential or ongoing litigation or investigations, composition of the corporation's investor base, shareholder engagement practices, shareholder campaigns, potential takeover approaches, its relationship with outside auditors, and its relationship with regulators. You may be asked to enter into a non-disclosure agreement before some of this information is shared by the corporation. You will want to attempt to determine if there are any particular industry- or corporation-specific risks or other factors that require special or immediate attention. Each corporation has different values and its own culture, mission, business model, operational complexity, and risk profile, tolerance, and appetite. A candidate's objective, independent views of these matters are instrumental both in deciding to join a board (or not) and in ongoing participation and effectiveness as a board member.

B. YOUR EVALUATION OF THE BOARD

You should seek to understand the board's track record and approach to effective oversight and long-term strategic planning, as well as its approach to decision making and leadership. There is no "one-size-fits-all" design for strong and effective corporate governance. You will want to spend time learning how the board is structured and operates based on publicly available documents that outline the corporation's governance, such as its proxy statement, board and committee governance documents, and codes of conduct.

Use discussions with the CEO and other directors to assess the board's independent oversight of the management team. Effective corporate governance requires that boards operate in a manner that is both independent of and at the same time cooperative and interactive with management. High-performing boards operate with a clear understanding of their role, responsibilities, and expectations and in a collegial fashion in which each director is fully engaged. Board candidates should seek a sense of the internal dynamics and information flow, as well as whether there are any areas of disagreement among the directors, between the directors and senior management, or among the members of senior management. Questions to ask may include the following:

- Does the board function with collegiality and a culture of constructive inquiry, respect for different viewpoints, and challenges? Do only a few directors ask questions, and do any directors tend to dominate the conversation?

- How has the board weathered past challenges or crises?
- Who are the board's internal and external advisors, including the general counsel and corporate secretary, and how accessible to directors are they? Do you feel confident that the board receives quality, timely, and meaningful information and advice to support its independent oversight role?
- Does the board know its role and the difference between the role of the board and the role of management?
- Is management open and transparent with the board, and does management communicate proactively with the board?
- What is the board's approach to, and frequency of, executive sessions?
- What is the board's approach to board evaluations and management succession planning?
- If any directors have recently left the board, what are their views of the corporation and what were the reasons for their departure?
- Most importantly, do you believe that senior management and the board have integrity and conduct themselves in a transparent, honest, and ethical manner?

Because directors must be able to work toward building consensus on complex issues in a fast-paced, dynamic operating environment, you should feel comfortable that you will be well-informed so that you can exercise your independent business judgment, openly share your views, and engage in constructive dialogue in an atmosphere of candor, mutual respect, and confidentiality.

C. YOUR ASSESSMENT OF YOUR CONTRIBUTION TO THE BOARD

It is prudent to reflect on your personal reasons, ability, and capacity to join and contribute to the board. Questions to ask may include the following:

- Is the opportunity to serve on this board sufficiently compelling to engage your serious interest and attention in light of competing commitments?
- Do you have sufficient time and flexibility to serve effectively, particularly if a corporate crisis or major transaction arises, taking into consideration the number of other boards on which you serve or, if you are an executive officer of a corporation, your duties as

an officer of that corporation? Will you be able to prepare for and attend board and committee meetings?

- Do you have any conflicts of interest with the corporation whose board you are considering joining or material relationships with the corporation, its senior management or other stakeholders, or its competitors? Are you prohibited from serving on the board because of the antitrust prohibitions on any person simultaneously serving as an officer or director of two competing corporations? Are there any personal, business, or other relationships that might give the appearance of an absence of independence from management?
- How frequently and where does the board meet, and do you have any known conflicts with the scheduled board and board committee meeting calendar?
- Do you have (or can you develop) a sufficient depth of understanding of the business (including its competitors, risks, and opportunities) to be an effective director?
- Does your employer or do other boards on which you serve have approval or notice requirements that must be considered before accepting a new board position?

D. THE BOARD'S EXPECTATIONS

You should also understand the board's expectations of you. Questions to ask may include the following:

- Is there a particular reason that the board has reached out to you? For example, does the board expect to rely on any particular professional expertise you may possess?
- Are there committees on which you will be expected to serve?
- What type of commitment is expected or required, in addition to onboarding and preparing for and attending meetings?

Expectations of board members have grown over time. Board members of public companies typically spend a significant amount of time preparing for and attending board meetings, board committee meetings, and other meetings related to board service.

E. OTHER EXPECTATIONS

Although the vast majority of public company directors are nominated by the incumbent board on behalf of all of the shareholders, some are nominated by the shareholders themselves. A nominee of a particular shareholder should consider that shareholder's expectations, the relationship of that shareholder to the corporation and other members of the board, and any ongoing relationship between the nominee and the shareholder. Additional concerns and processes will apply in the case of nominees in the context of a proxy contest. As discussed in Chapter 3, all directors—including those nominated by significant shareholders—have fiduciary duties to all shareholders.

F. COMPENSATION

Director compensation should be commensurate with the time and effort required and the risk undertaken. Public companies disclose their director compensation programs in their proxy statements, and the corporation should provide information to you so that you understand the program and any related requirements, such as share ownership guidelines, share retention requirements, and any ability to defer compensation. Investors generally expect that at least some director compensation will consist of equity. You should note, however, that even if directors are legally permitted to dispose of shares on the open market, directors are often strongly discouraged from doing so. Typically, all outside directors will be compensated in the same manner, with appropriate additional compensation for board and committee chairs and membership on certain time-intensive committees. You should consult your own tax advisor with respect to the form of compensation you will receive, as well as locations of meetings, to understand how it will fit within your personal financial and tax planning.

G. EXPOSURE

You should understand the legal framework that can create personal exposure for directors, as more fully described in other chapters of the *Guidebook*. Typically, the general counsel or corporate secretary will review with you the basic fiduciary duties and other legal requirements for directors. You should also request a copy (or summary) of insurance policies available to directors (directors and officers liability insurance, commonly referred to as D&O insurance) to ensure that the policies are up to date and provide appropriate coverage. It is advisable that you understand the corporation's protections for director exculpation from liability, indemnification rights, and legal expense advancement and how those protections apply in the context of potential and actual litigation or investigations. For public companies, a summary of this information can be found in Part II of the corporation's registration statement most recently filed with the SEC. You should consider the amount and scope of coverage provided by the corporation's D&O insurance, the quality of the corporation's insurance carrier(s), and whether the corporation has provided the outside directors with separate insurance (so-called Side A coverage) that is not also available to the corporation. Side A coverage can be complex and is generally insurance designed for directors to receive advancement of expenses and payment for settlements or judgments in the event the corporation cannot pay, due to financial constraints, limitations under law, or corporation governing documents. See Chapter 12 for additional information regarding D&O insurance.

During this diligence process, you should ask about the corporation's compliance, risk management, and internal controls as well as any significant investigations or claims involving the corporation, especially any that involve the activities of the board of directors, or any entity with which you are already affiliated. Where applicable, this review should also cover any industry-specific risk or exposure.

H. ONBOARDING

Director diligence does not end after a decision has been made for you to join the board; it continues throughout your board service. During the onboarding process, you should quickly gain a deeper understanding of the corporation's business and financial prospects so you can become an effective and engaged board member. Public companies typically have director orientation processes designed to ensure that new directors are quickly and fully versed in the strategy, financial condition, outlook, and material issues affecting the business and its operations, as well as to introduce new directors to a broad range of senior management personnel and provide opportunities to visit operational sites and facilities.

I. PRIVATE COMPANY BOARDS

The discussion in the *Guidebook* focuses on public company directors. Most directors of private companies will likely have some ownership interest in or connection to the corporation, its founders, or its owners. If you are asked to join the board of a private company or a closely controlled corporation, you should explore the expected role of an outsider on the board and understand the corporation's shareholder base (including any factions among the shareholders), business, reputation, and legal profile. In addition to the topics described in the *Guidebook* applicable to public companies, you should understand the directors' relationships with the corporation's shareholders. From your diligence, attempt to determine whether independent judgment is really desired and whether external legal, financial, or other advice will be available if requested (and, if so, from whom). You should also understand whether, and if applicable, when, a public offering of the corporation's securities is contemplated.

Part II:
Board Duties

CHAPTER

3 Duties of a Corporate Director

Under the corporation laws of most states, the board of directors is responsible for managing, or directing the management of, the business and affairs of the corporation. The board typically delegates operational responsibility to senior management, who are selected by the board or appointed under its authority. However, the board remains responsible for overseeing the conduct of the management of the corporation's business and affairs.

Directors fulfill their responsibilities through two primary board functions: decision making and oversight. Both the decision-making and oversight functions require directors to develop an understanding of the corporation's business, including the environment in which it operates and the risks and opportunities it faces. Thus, directors should ensure that they have sufficient information to engage in informed decision making and oversight.

Directors must exercise their responsibilities in the best interests of the corporation and its shareholders, and in doing so, directors should have in mind the interests of shareholders as a whole and not any particular shareholder. In addition, directors must satisfy legal standards governing their performance. Those responsibilities and legal obligations are discussed below.

A. RESPONSIBILITIES

1. Principal Board Functions

State corporation law emphasizes the board's responsibility to make major decisions on behalf of the corporation and to oversee its management. Major decisions include those that, under applicable statutes, the board *must* make (such as declaring dividends and electing officers) and *may* make (such as recommending changes to the bylaws). Board decisions may also include a wide range of matters not necessarily included in a statute, such as approval of business strategy, a major financing, or a new product or service.

The board's principal responsibilities are to:

- select the CEO and, in conjunction with the CEO, select senior management for the corporation;
- plan for CEO and other senior management succession;
- oversee the corporation's strategy; and
- identify and address potential opportunities, problems, and risks.

In all of its actions, the board should give significant consideration to, among other things, the corporation's strategy, including its financial and business objectives; its competitive environment; and its risk profile, tolerance, and appetite.

The board's other responsibilities will vary depending on the nature of the corporation and its business, but the board's other responsibilities typically include the following:

- monitoring performance in light of operating, financial, and other significant corporate plans, strategies, and objectives;
- approving major changes in plans and strategies;
- setting goals for the CEO and, in conjunction with the CEO, setting goals for other members of senior management;
- evaluating senior management performance and establishing, revising, and approving executive compensation;
- evaluating the board's leadership, committee structure, and composition, including implementing and maintaining a director refreshment process that considers the expertise and skills needed on the board, as well as independence, tenure, and diversity;
- implementing appropriate corporate governance policies and processes for the board and the corporation, and updating them as circumstances change and best practices evolve;
- understanding the risks that affect the corporation's business and reviewing and evaluating the corporation's risk tolerance, appetite, and management systems;

- understanding and approving the corporation's financial statements and disclosures and evaluating the adequacy of its internal controls over financial reporting and disclosure controls and procedures;
- evaluating and approving major transactions, such as mergers and acquisitions;
- monitoring and detecting fraud and encouraging employees to report misconduct;
- establishing and monitoring the effectiveness of systems for receiving and reporting information about the corporation's compliance with its legal and ethical obligations and the risks affecting its business;
- engaging with shareholders in coordination with management; and
- evaluating the board's own performance on a regular basis.

In performing its responsibilities, a board should be attentive to the following aspects of its duties:

a. Succession Planning

Boards are charged with overseeing succession planning, which is important both for unexpected emergencies and for the long term. Boards should develop, approve, and implement succession plans for the CEO and, in conjunction with the CEO, other members of senior management, including emergency plans for sudden management changes. Although there is no "one-size-fits-all" model for succession planning, the board's role is to assess on an ongoing basis whether current senior management is appropriate for the needs of the organization, as well as periodically review management development and succession plans. This process also allows directors to develop judgment about the corporation's potential future leaders.

Ongoing planning for what happens in the event of a vacancy in leadership is a critical board responsibility and is closely related to management development. The board should be aware of, and regularly reassess, how long the current CEO is likely to remain in office and what developments may cause a change in that expectation (including a shift in strategy, a change in performance, or an emergency or crisis). The board should also consider what might cause the CEO or other senior executive officers to contemplate leaving the corporation. Boards may look to the nominating and governance committee to support or lead this process, particularly in an emergency.

Succession planning rarely results in a hard and fast plan for a specific outcome. Two key components of succession planning are assessing and developing other management talent and considering what steps the CEO and other senior executive officers can take to further develop their own leadership capabilities and those of their direct reports. Decisions about succession planning and management development should also be coordinated with corporate strategy because the senior management team must have both an understanding of the corporate strategy and the ability to implement it.

The board should ensure the succession plan includes emergency procedures for management succession in the event of the unexpected death, disability, or departure of the CEO. The plan should also incorporate a review, with the CEO, of management's plans for the replacement of members of the senior management team, as well as the CEO's assessment of the ability of team members to lead, whether on an interim or longer basis, should the CEO be incapacitated.

The board should also engage in succession planning for board members.

b. Integrity and Reputation

The board safeguards the corporation's integrity and reputation both within and outside of the corporation and, together with the CEO, sets the "tone at the top." The CEO and senior management should take the lead in promoting integrity, honesty, and legal and ethical conduct throughout the organization. The board should continuously assess the CEO's performance in this area and set clear standards for ethical and legal behavior while encouraging appropriate values (including through policies and incentives). The board should also oversee the programs and procedures that management implements to promote compliance with law as well as ethical conduct and identify issues that may arise (including reporting mechanisms).

c. Shareholder Engagement

Increasingly, boards—and board committees or individual directors—engage in periodic communications with shareholders. Indeed, many institutional shareholders expect independent board leaders to be available for direct engagement. A shareholder's desire for engagement may evolve with corporate performance and changes in management and industry or market conditions. As a result, directors should be familiar with the corporation's shareholder base and, in coordination with management, be prepared to engage as needed.

Board efforts to enhance shareholder communication and dialogue require sensitivity to director confidentiality obligations as well as corporate policies and federal regulations regarding selective disclosure by public companies (Regulation FD). Individual directors are generally not authorized to speak on behalf of the corporation or the board, and absent specific authorization, individual directors should avoid responding to or communicating with any shareholders. Instead, management should coordinate these types of communications. This subject is discussed further under the heading "Legal Obligations—Other Obligations—Confidentiality."

d. Non-shareholder Constituencies

There is a growing recognition that boards should consider non-shareholder constituencies, including employees, suppliers, customers, the environment, and the communities in which the corporation operates. These groups are often referred to as "stakeholders." Some state corporation statutes expressly allow the board to consider the interests of stakeholders. Regardless of whether a corporation is governed by such statutes, stakeholder concerns can be considered in determining what is in the best interests of the corporation in most circumstances. Indeed, some institutional shareholders with significant, long-term investments in corporations increasingly expect boards to consider the interests of all stakeholders. Being responsive to stakeholder interests and concerns can contribute positively to corporate valuation, workplace culture, and reputation for integrity and ethical behavior. However, a board has certain duties, especially in some "change of control" contexts, which may require prioritizing shareholder interests, and in any event, a board must focus on the best interests of the corporation and its shareholders. See Chapter 6 for further discussion of this topic.

2. Director Effectiveness

Understanding the corporation's business, operations, products, and competitive environment is fundamental to a director's oversight and decision-making responsibilities. Accordingly, a director's understanding of the corporation and its industry should include:

- the corporation's overall strategy and business plan;
- the key drivers of the corporation's profitability and cash flow—how the corporation makes and uses money, both as a whole and also in significant business segments;

- the corporation's operational and financial plans, strategies, objectives, and approach to further enhancing shareholder value;
- the corporation's economic, financial, regulatory, and competitive risks, as well as risks to the corporation's physical assets, information systems, intellectual property, personnel, and reputation;
- the corporation's financial condition and the results of its operations, including those of its significant business segments for recent periods;
- the corporation's performance compared with that of its competitors; and
- the corporation's economic, environmental, and social sustainability.

In addition, each director should be satisfied that effective systems exist for timely reporting to, and consideration by, the board or relevant board committees of the following:

- corporate objectives and strategic plans;
- current business and financial performance, including significant business segments, as compared to board-approved objectives and plans;
- material risk and liability contingencies, including industry, cybersecurity, and reputational risk, as well as current and threatened litigation, product liability issues, and regulatory matters;
- human capital management, employee welfare, and safety concerns; and
- control systems designed to manage risk and to provide reasonable assurance of compliance with law and corporate policies, including misconduct.

Directors should do their homework and review board and committee agendas and related materials in advance of meetings so that they are prepared to participate actively and on an informed basis in board activities. In addition to attending board and committee meetings, directors should ensure the minutes accurately reflect what occurred at meetings and that identified action items are being pursued. Directors should also be informed about the activities of board committees on which they do not serve. Indeed, staying informed is a continuing responsibility between meetings, not just in preparing for them.

Directors should have an attitude of constructive skepticism and should not be reticent or passive. To be a director means to direct, including:

- participating on an informed basis;
- asking questions;

- listening to other directors and senior management;
- challenging management as appropriate;
- applying considered business judgment to matters brought before the board; and
- when necessary, bringing other matters to the full board's attention.

B. LEGAL OBLIGATIONS

Directors must meet certain legal standards governing their conduct. In addition to the two fundamental duties of care and loyalty, directors must satisfy obligations of inquiry, confidentiality, and disclosure (or candor), all of which are addressed in this section. Each director works for the benefit of the corporation, regardless of how that director was nominated or elected. Directors may take notice of the interests of particular shareholders when performing their decision-making and oversight duties, but they must each act in a manner they reasonably believe to be in the best interests of the corporation and its shareholders as a whole.

1. Care

A director's duty of care primarily relates to the responsibility to be informed and attentive in making decisions and overseeing the corporation's business. Typically, the duty of care is articulated as the duty to act in good faith, with the care that a reasonable person in a similar position and circumstance would exercise and in a manner the director reasonably believes to be in the best interests of the corporation and its shareholders. To satisfy the duty of care, directors should consider the following:

a. Time Commitment and Regular Attendance

Directors should commit the required time to prepare for, regularly attend, and participate in board and committee meetings. According to state corporation law, directors cannot participate or vote by proxy; personal participation is required. The availability of high-quality videoconference equipment has made videoconferences, rather than audio-only teleconferences, a staple in the conduct of board and committee meetings, especially off-cycle ones. As a result, remote participation for directors is now more effective than in the past. Nevertheless, directors who are physically present at a meeting can engage in spontaneous interactions that occur before, during, and after the meeting and are generally more aware of the group's dynamics than when participating remotely. As a result, many boards strongly prefer in-person meetings.

b. Need to Be Informed and Prepared

Directors must be reasonably informed, meaning they must both (1) have reasonably available material information relevant to the decision being made and (2) consider that information and its sufficiency. Whether information is relevant to a decision is itself a matter entrusted to the business judgment of directors. Without sufficient information and preparation, directors cannot participate meaningfully or fulfill their duties effectively. In most cases, the best source of information about the corporation is management. As a result, directors often ask some management members to be present at board or committee meetings. To be informed and prepared, a director should:

- read board materials in advance of meetings;
- make sure that management provides sufficient information about the corporation's business and affairs;
- request additional information when appropriate;
- ask questions of management or advisors to understand and/or clarify the information provided and any action contemplated;
- request legal or other expert advice when appropriate for a board decision; and
- if the information available is insufficient, consider delaying action.

Directors should establish expectations about the timeliness of information provided, appreciating that under some circumstances, information cannot be provided well in advance of a board meeting. In the absence of significant time constraints, however, directors should receive the relevant information sufficiently in advance of the board or committee meeting to be able to study and reflect on it.

2. Loyalty

The duty of loyalty requires directors to act in good faith and avoid or appropriately manage conflicts of interest. Situations implicating loyalty to the corporation include:

- the failure to act in good faith;
- personal or financial conflicts of interest with the corporation;
- disloyalty for reasons other than personal or financial conflicts of interest; and
- the improper "taking" of corporate opportunities.

a. Good Faith

The duty of good faith encompasses what is commonly known as the oversight duty as well as ensuring that directors do not act in bad faith or intentionally or knowingly disregard duties or responsibilities. Directors must have a good faith belief that their actions are in the best interests of the corporation and its shareholders. In overseeing risk as well as corporate management and decision making, good faith requires directors to ask questions and question answers. Directors are entitled to rely on management, experts (like auditors), and board committees. Thus, the oversight role requires developing industry- and company-specific knowledge that allows directors to rely in good faith on reports provided.

Questions about good faith usually arise after the fact when harm occurs, and although hindsight can be 20/20, it is not the measure for oversight. Instead, the focus is on what a reasonable director, engaging in a thoughtful and focused manner, would have done. As discussed below in the section on the business judgment rule, only director choices and decisions, and not the failure to decide, are protected. A director may fail to act in good faith in a variety of ways, including the following:

- intentionally acting with a purpose other than advancing the corporation's best interests;
- failing to act when there is a known duty to act;
- acting with a conscious disregard of or extreme inattention to director duties;
- acting with the intent to violate, or with intentional disregard of, an applicable law;
- consciously disregarding internal controls, risk management, or monitoring and compliance systems; or
- intentionally or consciously disregarding "red flags," including signs that there is or might be wrongdoing in the organization, a toxic culture, or persistent gaps in information across the organization.

b. Conflicts of Interest

Directors can violate their duty of loyalty by using their positions for personal profit or gain or for any other personal or noncorporate advantage. Instead, they should be alert and sensitive to any interest they (or close family members, friends, or affiliates) may have that might conflict, or even appear to conflict, with the best interests of the corporation and its shareholders. Transactions involving a conflict of interest are sometimes unavoidable and are not inherently improper. However, they must be managed appropriately, which usually includes disclosure of the material facts to the board or a committee and to the general counsel.

There are several common types of conflicts of interest, including:

- when a director has an interest in a matter that is before the board for decision, including a contract or transaction to which the corporation is or is proposed to be a party, that involves the use of corporate assets, or that may involve competition with the corporation;
- when a person related to or affiliated with a director has an interest in the transaction that could impair the director's ability to be impartial in considering the transaction; and
- when directors owe a duty of confidentiality to a third party that impairs or prohibits full disclosure of certain information.

Best practices for directors with conflicts in these situations include:

- disclosing to their fellow directors the conflict and all other pertinent information and responding to questions;
- recusing themselves from the discussion about the matter, thus enabling discussion without the appearance of or actual influence by the interested director; and
- remaining out of the room and abstaining from any vote on the matter.

Disinterested directors (meaning independent directors who have no stake in the decision), a special committee of disinterested directors, or, if needed, shareholders, may authorize a conflicted transaction provided that they receive full disclosure of material information about the transaction and the conflict. In reviewing a transaction, the disinterested directors should determine whether:

- the proposed transaction is in the best interests of the corporation and its shareholders;
- the terms of the proposed transaction are at least as favorable to the corporation as those that might be available from unrelated persons or entities; and
- the process by which the decision is approved or ratified is fair.

In deciding whether to approve a conflicted transaction, disinterested directors often find independent advice helpful. This advice may be contained in:

- oral or written fairness opinions, appraisals, or valuations by investment bankers or appraisers;
- legal advice or opinions on various issues; or
- analyses, reports, or recommendations by other relevant experts.

These procedures both safeguard the corporation and any interested director and protect the enforceability of any action taken. They should also be documented in board minutes. Disinterested approval thus acts as a cleansing mechanism for the transaction. In its absence, a board's decision may be subject to the entire fairness standard of judicial review, which is the most stringent level of review and requires a demonstration that the price was fair to the corporation and that the transaction process was fair to the corporation.

Finally, a transaction between a director, or a member of the director's immediate family, and the corporation is a "related person" transaction under the federal securities laws and may require disclosure in a public company's annual report, proxy statement, or other public filings. Even if the transaction does not require public disclosure, the corporation may be required to disclose in general terms whether the board considered the transaction in determining whether the director is an "independent" director under applicable U.S. stock exchange listing standards. In addition, corporations may have their own policies in these areas, and waiving such a policy for a director may trigger a disclosure obligation under the federal securities laws. Directors should consider seeking the advice of experienced counsel and be familiar with these disclosure requirements and related corporate policies, including whether the transaction must be disclosed in the corporation's financial statements.

c. *Corporate Opportunities*

When an opportunity related to the business of the corporation, including its subsidiaries and affiliates, becomes available to a director, state law may prohibit the director from "taking" the opportunity without first offering it to or consulting with the corporation and obtaining the corporation's consent. Even where state law does not prohibit directors from taking such opportunities, directors typically make such opportunities available to the corporation before they pursue them. Indeed, as with other conflicts of interest, full disclosure and a proper process can help directors avoid liability and relieve directors from the burden of proving that they were not disloyal.

Whether directors should first offer an opportunity to the corporation will depend on several factors. These factors include whether the opportunity is similar to the corporation's existing or contemplated business, the circumstances under which the director learned of the opportunity, and whether the corporation may have an interest or expectancy in the opportunity. Some state corporation statutes provide that the corporation's articles or certificate of incorporation may include a provision limiting or eliminating a director's duty to offer the specified opportunities or categories of opportunities to the corporation.

Generally, if a director has reason to believe that a contemplated transaction might be a corporate opportunity, the director should consider bringing it to the attention of the board and disclose all known material information about the opportunity. If the board (acting through its disinterested directors) or the shareholders disclaim interest in the opportunity on behalf of the corporation, then the director is free to pursue it.

3. Other Obligations

a. Inquiry

Under both the duty of care and the duty of loyalty, directors should inquire into potential problems or issues when alerted by circumstances or events suggesting attention is appropriate. For example, inquiry is warranted when conflicts of interest exist; when information appears materially inaccurate or inadequate; when there is reason to question the competence, loyalty, or candor of management or an advisor; or when common sense calls for inquiry or skepticism.

When directors have information indicating that the corporation is or may be experiencing significant problems in a particular area of business or may be engaging in potentially unlawful or unethical conduct, they should inquire further and follow up until reasonably satisfied that management is addressing the situation. Even absent such red flags, directors should periodically satisfy themselves that the corporation maintains information systems and procedures appropriately designed to identify and manage risks and reasonably effective in maintaining compliance with laws and corporate policies and procedures.

b. Confidentiality

Directors must keep confidential material matters involving the corporation that have not been disclosed to the public. Directors must be aware of and comply with the corporation's confidentiality and disclosure policies. Although public company directors may receive inquiries from major shareholders, media, analysts, or friends, individual directors should avoid responding to such inquiries in the absence of a specific understanding with the full board, particularly when confidential or market-sensitive information is involved. Instead, they should refer requests for information to the CEO or other corporate spokesperson.

Confidentiality concerns also arise with directors who have been appointed to a board pursuant to an agreement or understanding with a particular shareholder. A well-drafted confidentiality agreement between the corporation and the shareholder governing if, when, and how such information may be shared can protect the corporation, the shareholder, and the director. Whether an individual director may share confidential information with shareholders who nominate or elect the director (subject to selective disclosure and insider trading prohibitions) will depend on:

- the situation, including whether the corporation or board expects that information will be shared;
- the type of information at issue (e.g., whether it is privileged);
- the harm the shared information might cause to the corporation; and
- the potential adversity of the shareholder's interest to the corporation.

A director who improperly discloses non-public information to persons outside the corporation may:

- harm the corporation's competitive position or damage investor relations;
- incur personal liability as a tipper of material inside information;
- cause the corporation to violate federal securities laws (in particular, Regulation FD);
- damage the bond of trust between and among directors and management; and
- discourage candid discussions and jeopardize boardroom effectiveness and director collaboration.

Notably, board meeting discussions and dynamics are confidential. Directors should ensure that they do not discuss those matters with non-directors. Indeed, even board meeting dates and locations may be confidential, and directors should pay attention to and be aware of any confidentiality concerns surrounding those matters.

c. *Disclosure (or Candor)*

1. To Shareholders

Directors should never mislead or misinform shareholders and should speak with candor. In addition, directors have an obligation to provide shareholders with all relevant material information when presenting them with a voting or investment decision.

2. To Directors

An effective board process depends on mutual trust among directors and a collegial atmosphere that encourages candor among directors and between the board and management. Generally, directors should inform other directors and management about information material to the board's performance of its responsibilities. Where a director has legal or other duties of confidentiality owed to another person, the director should seek legal advice regarding the director's obligations, including reporting any confidentiality obligations to the other directors and, in some circumstances, not participating in consideration of the matter.

C. JUDICIAL REVIEW OF BOARD DECISIONS

1. Business Judgment Rule

The business judgment rule normally governs judicial review of board decisions. It is a standard for analyzing director conduct—not a description of a duty—to determine whether a board decision may be challenged, or a director will be personally liable. Importantly, the business judgment rule applies only when fiduciaries make a decision, which includes a decision not to take action. But it does not apply when fiduciaries fail to engage and make a decision.

If the business judgment rule applies, a judge will presume that, in making a business decision, independent and disinterested directors acted on an informed basis, in good faith, and with the honest belief that the action taken was in the best interests of the corporation and its shareholders. In certain situations, in particular relating to change-of-control or conflict transactions, courts will apply two more stringent levels of review. See Chapter 6 for a discussion of these standards.

2. Right to Rely on Others

In discharging board or committee duties, directors may rely in good faith on reports, opinions, information, and statements (including financial statements and other financial data) from:

- corporate officers or employees the director reasonably believes to be reliable and competent in the matters presented;
- experts (legal counsel, certified public accountants, or others) on matters that the director reasonably believes to be within the expert's professional competence or as to which the person otherwise merits confidence; and
- board committees on which the director does not serve, if the director reasonably believes that the committee merits confidence.

This reliance is permissible unless the director has knowledge that would make the reliance unwarranted. Delegation to a committee does not relieve a director of oversight responsibility. Instead, depending on the scope of the committee's authority, a director may need to stay informed about committee activities.

Directors also implicitly rely on each other's statements, good faith, and judgment in making decisions for the corporation's benefit. Indeed, directors are expected to use their knowledge, experience, and special expertise for the benefit of all directors and the corporation generally. Thus, reliance is particularly likely when some directors have substantial experience or expertise in an area germane to the corporation's business (e.g., by having specialized knowledge about a particular industry).

Directors should not, however, cede responsibility to any other director for board matters. Rather, directors should use the information relied upon as one element of their judgment. A director does not want to be in the position of saying, "I voted for the matter because another director said it was okay."

Obtaining input from competent advisors is also a hallmark of a careful decision-making process. Accordingly, directors who rely in good faith on advisors, professionals, and other persons with particular expertise or competence generally enjoy broad protections from liability. Relying in good faith requires that directors reasonably believe that the advice is within the person's area of competence and that the person was selected with reasonable care.

D. DIRECTOR RIGHTS

Directors have both legal and customary rights of access to the information and resources needed to perform their responsibilities and meet legal standards of conduct. This information is important to ensure that directors are able to perform their fiduciary duties. This right, of course, is accompanied by the duty to keep that information confidential and not to misuse information for personal benefit or for the benefit of others.

Among the most important are the rights to:

- inspect books and records;
- request additional information reasonably necessary to exercise informed oversight and make careful decisions;
- inspect facilities to gain an understanding of corporate operations;
- receive timely notice of all meetings in which a director is entitled to participate;
- receive copies of key documents and of all board and committee meeting minutes; and
- receive regular oral or written reports of the activities of all board committees.

In addition, directors generally have access to key executives, other employees of the corporation, the corporation's general counsel, and other advisors to obtain information relevant to the performance of their duties. Importantly, the general counsel's client is the corporation, as represented by the board of directors, and not the CEO, any individual director, or any other officer or group of managers. The board and board committees should also have access to the corporation's regular outside counsel, if one exists, and, if needed, the authority to retain their own legal counsel and professional advisors, independent of those who usually advise the corporation.

Directors may (and should) request that any issue of concern be put on the board (or appropriate committee) agenda.

CHAPTER

4 Risk Oversight and Compliance

Oversight of risk management and legal compliance are critical components of the board's responsibilities. Well-publicized financial, operational, legal, and security failures in recent years have led to a heightened focus on the role of the board with respect to these matters. The board's oversight function includes working with management to identify material risks and determine the corporation's risk tolerance. The board also oversees the development of effective risk management and legal compliance programs.

A. AREAS OF RISK FACING CORPORATIONS

An understanding of the material internal and external risks potentially affecting a corporation is essential for a board's oversight of the corporation's business and affairs. This includes a full understanding of relevant contingencies, threats, and vulnerabilities. With this background, management and the board can determine the corporation's risk tolerance and appetite.

Risks affecting corporations typically fall into three broad categories: business, legal, and reputational. Business risks frequently include failures of internal controls over financial reporting, breaches of physical plant or data security, product quality and safety issues, intellectual property protection, and political developments or natural disasters that impact business continuity.

Cybersecurity and climate change impact risks are other common business risks that have received significant attention from regulators and investors. Although virtually all corporations face cyber risks, some businesses are more exposed than others. For example, corporations with access to large amounts of personal consumer information may be especially tempting targets for data theft. Security breaches, data theft, loss of proprietary or commercially sensitive information, and infrastructure damage can severely disrupt the corporation's business and cause financial losses and reputational damage.

Legal compliance failures are another important risk category for a corporation. As with business risks, the nature of a corporation's operations affects its exposure to legal risks. Corporations operating in multiple jurisdictions face more complex compliance risks than those that operate in one jurisdiction.

Business and legal risk management failures may cause serious reputational damage to the corporation. For example, a failure of a corporation's internal controls can result in a misstatement of revenues, a requirement to restate financial statements, possible disciplinary actions, associated negative publicity, and litigation. Health, safety, environmental protection, product safety, and human rights issues increasingly drive consumer and investor behavior, business partner decisions, employee morale, and business reputation. As such, they are not only matters of legal compliance, but they are also matters of legitimate public concern. A major product failure, data theft, or inappropriate or unlawful conduct by executives, such as sexual harassment or personal use of corporate assets, also present especially inviting topics for news media. They may also present risks to the long-term success of the corporation.

B. THE BOARD'S OVERSIGHT ROLE

Risk management includes identifying and assessing risks, considering mitigating factors, implementing risk controls, ongoing monitoring, and taking action in response to any "red flags." Although boards are generally not involved in day-to-day risk management, their oversight role includes active involvement in strategic decision making and establishing and articulating the corporation's culture with respect to risk, setting expectations relating to risk, and establishing consequences for failures in risk management through an effective compliance program.

1. The Basis for the Board's Responsibilities

As explained in Chapter 3, the board's core oversight duties are a component of the duty of loyalty. The seminal *Caremark* case from Delaware in 1996 set a high bar for oversight liability, requiring a "sustained or systematic failure" or disregard of "red flags." However, in recent years, courts have permitted more of these so-called "*Caremark* claims" to proceed against directors for failures to give sufficient board-level attention to mission-critical risks, thus highlighting the need for directors to engage in active oversight of risk (including through the implementation of an information and reporting system) and ensure that the corporation keeps sufficient records of their review and response to risks.

In addition to its duties under state and other laws, a public company board will need to observe SEC disclosure rules, which implicitly highlight the risk management responsibilities of the board. SEC regulations, for instance, require public companies to disclose the extent and structure of the board's role in risk oversight. Perceived board failures to address risk management effectively could lead to criticism from institutional and activist investors and to proxy advisory firms recommending votes against directors.

2. The Role of Board Committees

Board committees can play an important role in risk oversight. Assessment and monitoring of certain types of risks may be more suited to the expertise of a particular committee, or the use of a particular committee may be mandated by law or U.S. stock exchange listing standards. For example, federal law requires certain financial institutions to establish risk committees of the board that include at least one risk management expert. In addition, NYSE listing standards mandate that the duties of the audit committee include discussion of the listed company's major financial risk exposures and the steps management has taken to monitor and control such exposures. Also, the compensation committee of a public company must consider whether the corporation's compensation policies and practices encourage excessive risk taking. The responsibilities of each board committee often include understanding and addressing the issues relating to risk relevant to that committee's areas of oversight.

3. Board Decision Making

One of the board's most important responsibilities is to engage with senior management as it develops the corporation's overall business management and strategic plans. In working with management to establish and periodically review strategy, the board should consider the risks and advantages inherent in a particular strategy, risks of pursuing one strategy over another, potential risks that may affect a strategy, and external variables that may change the risks associated with a strategy. The board should understand the views of shareholders, auditors, and regulatory authorities on the corporation's critical risk matters.

Although the board's role is primarily one of oversight, the board may want to take a more active role in areas of executive compensation and other transactions with senior executives where there are inherent conflicts or there may be an appearance of conflict between the interests of the corporation and the senior executives. Similarly, the board may need to become actively involved in risk management when it becomes aware that events have occurred that could be attributed to a management failure to manage risk. These events could include major accidents, regulatory fines, business interruptions, or lawsuits by employees or third parties that threaten material economic or reputational harm to the corporation.

4. Oversight of Implementation and Effectiveness

Once risk tolerance and overall business strategies have been established, the board should exercise its oversight role to ensure that management's design and implementation of risk management policies are consistent with the established risk tolerance and strategies. The board should satisfy itself that appropriate systems and processes are in place to identify, monitor, control, and, when appropriate, accept, or seek to avoid or mitigate, risk and to make necessary or desirable disclosures. An effective risk management program identifies the most significant vulnerabilities facing the corporation and is updated periodically to address changes in the risk environment.

The board should also be satisfied that the corporation has both the internal and external resources and appropriately skilled personnel to effectively implement and drive compliance with risk management policies. To assist the board and management, some corporations designate a chief risk officer or create a high-level management committee that reports regularly to the board or a board committee.

The board, and its relevant committees, should receive periodic reports from senior management and risk management personnel about the corporation's risk management activities and significant risk incidents. It is good practice for the board as a whole and committees with risk oversight responsibilities to meet periodically in executive session with the chief risk officer or other risk management personnel. The board or committee should agree with management on the frequency, content, and form in which risk oversight information is provided to the board and appropriate committees.

The board's oversight responsibilities extend to monitoring the effectiveness of the corporation's risk management policies and procedures. For example, the board could periodically review the corporation's preparedness and response plans for a cyber incident. Such evaluation can be enhanced, for example, by assuring that management periodically conducts an incident response "tabletop" exercise in which managers or independent experts assess, and perhaps even attack, the corporation's systems and then report to the board on the conclusions reached and any improvements to be made as a result of the exercise.

The board should work with management to establish measurable goals to assess effectiveness. The board's risk management oversight should be forward-looking with respect to strategy, product innovations, cyclical risks, and emerging issues. The board will want to be comfortable that the corporation's policies encourage prompt reporting of significant risk incidents to senior management and the board or appropriate board committee.

5. Crisis Management

Effective management of disclosure and publicity regarding a failure of risk management is key to limiting the adverse impact of unanticipated events. The board should periodically consider the most likely crises the corporation may face and review whether the corporation has an effective crisis management plan in place for each of these potential crises. Good crisis management programs include advance identification of members of the crisis management team, assignment of appropriate crisis management roles for key officers, procedures for prompt notification of the board, and a plan for public communications and regulatory filings related to the crisis. Board-level monitoring of these programs can provide an objective review of management's plans for response to a crisis and help ensure that the board is appropriately informed when that time comes.

The board's role will generally become more active when a crisis occurs, often providing more active support to management. If senior management's conduct is an issue in the crisis situation, board members may move from an oversight role to one of direct engagement in management. For example, the board may need to designate a manager who is not a target of criticism, or appoint a director or board committee, to step into the role of managing the corporation's response.

C. COMPLIANCE

A well-conceived and properly implemented compliance program can significantly reduce the incidence of legal and corporate policy violations and consequent risks. For example, although the federal sentencing guidelines impose significant penalties on corporations found guilty of criminal violations, they also provide for meaningful reductions in sanctions for corporations that demonstrate they have effective programs in place to prevent and detect such violations.

Boards should ensure that the corporation has written policies designed to promote compliance with law and corporate policy and for regular training of management and employees to comply with such policies. The U.S. stock exchanges require listed companies to adopt codes of business conduct applicable to all employees, officers, and directors. The corporation should have controls throughout the organization for monitoring compliance with its codes and relevant laws as well as a regular program of mandatory compliance training for its employees. Federal law and SEC regulations require anonymous reporting procedures with respect to financial reporting and controls issues. The board should be satisfied that an effective process is in place to enable such anonymous reports in a manner that protects the reporting employee from retaliation and provides the board or relevant committees with regular information about reported matters and how they were resolved.

The board or appropriate board committee can review compliance policies periodically for effectiveness and currency, including the content, depth, and frequency of training. Many public companies assign compliance oversight to the audit committee. With the increased burdens placed on public company audit committees, however, some boards have formed a separate compliance or legal affairs committee. The board and relevant committees generally meet regularly with the compliance and legal officers to be briefed on ongoing compliance matters, pending or threatened claims, and potential future risks.

D. DISCLOSURE COMPLIANCE

A public company's disclosure documents (e.g., annual reports, quarterly reports, current reports, proxy statements, prospectuses, earnings releases, and investor presentations) must fairly present and not omit material information about the corporation and its business, financial condition, results, prospects, and risks. Management is responsible for drafting and preparing the corporation's disclosures. Many public companies establish management disclosure committees with responsibility for preparing the corporation's SEC filings and other public financial disclosures. Although management has primary responsibility for a corporation's financial statements and other public disclosures, the board through its audit committee has oversight responsibility over all financial disclosures. The board should assure itself that the corporation's procedures for identifying matters requiring disclosure and preparing disclosure documents are reasonably designed to produce accurate and complete public disclosures in an appropriate and timely manner. In addition to the disclosure documents requiring their signatures, directors should be familiar with all of the corporation's significant disclosure documents and ensure that those documents convey all material information about the business in a legally compliant and timely manner. Disclosure requirements for public companies are further addressed in Chapter 5.

CHAPTER

5 Duties under the Federal Securities Laws

Federal and state laws regulate the disclosure practices and securities transactions of public companies and their directors, officers, and employees. The federal securities laws, administered by the SEC, affect many activities of public companies. Violation of these laws may result in civil and criminal penalties, imposed not only on the corporation but also potentially on individual directors and officers. Directors need to be attentive to their own, as well as the corporation's, compliance with these laws. Review of programs and policies designed to maintain compliance with the federal securities laws is often delegated to the board's audit committee or to another committee assigned specific responsibilities for legal compliance.

A. SEC REPORTING REQUIREMENTS

Public companies must file both periodic and current reports with the SEC. Periodic reports are an annual report on Form 10-K and quarterly reports on Form 10-Q for each of the first three fiscal quarters. Current reports on Form 8-K are required for disclosure of specified events that are presumptively significant, including quarterly earnings releases, entry into or amendment to material contracts, changes in the board and senior management, and voting results of shareholder meetings. A public company may also use Form 8-K for voluntary disclosure of other information. The SEC's proxy rules require that the annual meeting proxy statement be accompanied or preceded by an annual report to shareholders.

The corporation's annual report on Form 10-K contains the prior fiscal year's audited financial statements, as well as a business description, risk factors, management's discussion and analysis of the corporation's results of operations and financial condition, and a description of important trends and uncertainties. The Form 10-K is the most detailed of the reports companies file with the SEC, and it must be signed by the company, specified officers, and a majority of the corporation's directors. Separate and apart from the audit committee's involvement with the financial statements and related certifications, all directors should review and be satisfied with the corporate processes used to prepare the Form 10-K and understand the significant disclosures in that report. Therefore, the full board should have an opportunity to read, comment on, and ask questions about the Form 10-K before it is filed.

Public companies must maintain effective systems of internal controls and procedures for collecting, reviewing, and disclosing financial and other material information about the corporation. Management of larger public companies must annually evaluate and attest to the effectiveness of the corporation's internal control over financial reporting, with a requirement that the independent auditor attest to such effectiveness. The board, generally through its audit committee, will want to receive and examine reports about each of these reviews. The audit committee should receive regular reports on the effectiveness of internal controls and of any deficiencies in those controls that management or the independent auditor identifies. Material weaknesses in internal controls must be reported in public filings, and the audit committee should oversee the related remediation efforts.

Directors are not expected to verify the accuracy of underlying facts contained in earnings releases or reports filed with the SEC, but they should be satisfied that the disclosures are not contrary to the facts as they know them. In addition, the audit committee and the full board should be satisfied that there are disclosure controls and procedures in place reasonably designed to achieve the timeliness, accuracy, and completeness of the disclosures required to be filed in SEC reports. In addition to the attestation regarding internal controls described above, the CEO and Chief Financial Officer (CFO) of a public company are required to review and, based on their knowledge, certify the material accuracy and completeness of quarterly and annual reports. Audit committee members of a public company should be familiar with these certifications and the procedures undertaken to support them.

B. PROXY STATEMENTS

Public companies soliciting proxies for shareholder votes on the election of directors and other matters must furnish each shareholder with a proxy statement. In most cases, the corporation files only the final proxy statement, as distributed to shareholders. However, if actions other than an uncontested election of directors or other routine business are to be taken, the corporation must file a preliminary proxy statement with the SEC, which may review and comment on it. It is good practice for every director to review a reasonably close-to-final draft of the proxy statement before it is filed with the SEC, particularly sections dealing with matters about which the director has personal knowledge or containing a report of a committee on which the director serves.

The proxy statement for the annual shareholder meeting must include information about the corporation's directors, executive officers, and greater than five percent shareholders, as well as about certain governance policies. For directors in particular, the proxy statement must include disclosure about each director's and director nominee's experience, qualifications, attributes, or skills that led the board to conclude that the person should serve as a director of the corporation. The proxy statement must also include information about the corporation's compensation of its executive officers and directors, including a discussion of the corporation's compensation objectives, policies, and practices. Finally, the proxy statement must include information about related person transactions, covering not only transactions with directors but also transactions with immediate family members of directors and entities controlled by directors. Corporations will typically request information for these disclosures through an annual director and officer questionnaire. The applicable rules are detailed and technical, and directors should consult the corporation's legal counsel about the requirements.

In addition to the items on which management is seeking a shareholder vote, SEC rules also require public companies to include in the proxy statement proposals that shareholders have submitted for a shareholder vote (so long as the proposing shareholders have satisfied applicable requirements). These proposals, which are often fiercely contested, typically involve governance or environmental, social, and governance (ESG) matters.

C. REGISTRATION STATEMENTS

Directors should pay special attention to the accuracy of the registration statements the corporation files with the SEC in connection with any public offering of securities (including in a merger or acquisition). A majority of the corporation's directors must sign registration statements, but regardless of whether a director signs the registration statement, all directors are liable for material inaccuracies or omissions in the registration statement unless they establish that, after due diligence, they were not aware of the inaccuracy or omission.

The director's primary defense to registration statement liability is known as the "due diligence" defense. To benefit from this defense, directors must show that, after reasonable investigation, they had reasonable grounds to believe and did believe that the registration statement did not contain any materially false statements or omit any information required to make what was said not misleading. Actions required by a director to satisfy the due diligence standard will vary with the circumstances. Each director should personally review the registration statement for accuracy, with particular attention to those statements and disclosures in the registration statement that are within the director's knowledge and competence. During the registration process, directors should satisfy themselves that the corporation has developed and used appropriate corporate disclosure controls and procedures reasonably designed to ensure the registration statement's accuracy and completeness. Although all registration statements should be prepared with appropriate care, certain registered offerings may have a higher potential for liability than others, such as an initial public offering, a follow-on equity offering, a large acquisition using the corporation's stock, or a financing or reorganization of a public company that has experienced problems. Accordingly, a board will want to obtain the benefit of a review of the disclosures in the registration statement with counsel, accountants, and management present before the filing of registration statements for such offerings.

Often, the disclosures in the corporation's Form 10-K and other reports filed previously with the SEC are incorporated into the registration statement. Therefore, the procedures used to review these reports are also important, particularly when it is likely the corporation will conduct a registered securities offering. In this regard, directors may also want to consider consulting with the corporation's securities counsel to understand any material changes made to disclosure documents in response to SEC comments and to confirm that the process followed is intended to fulfill the requirements for the due diligence defense.

D. TRANSACTIONS IN CORPORATION SECURITIES

Various federal securities laws and SEC rules apply to transactions that a director conducts in the corporation's securities. Although most public companies assist directors in complying with these responsibilities, these obligations are the director's, and violations may subject the director to personal liability. It is important, therefore, for a director to be generally familiar with the applicable laws and rules and to seek qualified legal counsel to assist in compliance when appropriate.

1. Insider Trading

The federal securities laws—most notably, Exchange Act Rule 10b-5—prohibit corporate insiders, including directors, and the corporation itself from purchasing or selling securities, either on the open market or in private transactions, when they possess material information about the corporation that has not been publicly disclosed or that otherwise has not been disclosed to the counterparty. The corporation or an insider in possession of such information may not buy or sell the corporation's securities until the information has been publicly disseminated. The federal securities laws also prohibit insiders from "tipping" (i.e., revealing material non-public information, or giving a recommendation to buy or sell, to friends, family members, or others who trade based upon such information). Under Rule 10b5-1, directors and other insiders can mitigate the risk of insider trading liability by adopting plans, for scheduled sales or purchases of the corporation's securities, at a time when they have no material non-public information.

Information is material if there is a substantial likelihood that a reasonable investor would consider it important because it significantly alters the total mix of information about the corporation. Examples of material information include:

- financial results of a completed fiscal period;
- significant acquisitions or divestitures;
- important business developments, such as results of an important clinical trial for a pharmaceutical company; and
- the establishment, increase, or reduction of a dividend on a corporation's stock.

If there is any doubt whether undisclosed information is material, an insider should seek legal guidance, and, when there is doubt, directors should err on the side of treating the information as material.

Violation of insider trading laws can trigger strict sanctions—both civil and criminal. Criminal liability can involve fines and imprisonment. The violator (i.e., the trader, the tipper, or the tippee) is liable for any profit made or loss avoided. In addition, a court can assess a penalty of treble damages (i.e., three times the profits made or losses avoided). The SEC and the stock exchanges have aggressive programs of discovering and proceeding against insider trading violations. The SEC may award "whistleblowers" who report a violation a percentage of the amount of the penalty recovered. In addition, the SEC can prohibit any individual who has violated the insider trading laws from serving as an officer or director of any public company.

Most public companies have policies that address insider trading, many of which require senior executives and directors to contact a designated person before trading in the corporation's securities (or making gifts) so that any proposed transaction can be reviewed in light of the current state of public information and the corporation's internal policies. Many of these policies require that insiders and their affiliates transact in the corporation's securities only during specific "window periods" and prohibit trading during specified "blackout" periods around earnings releases and other material events. Although corporations are not liable for their insiders' violations of the insider trading laws, they have an interest in establishing and enforcing policies that will help avoid the reputational harm that can occur when insiders violate the law.

2. Public Sales of Securities

The SEC considers a director to be a "controlling person" of the corporation. As a result, sales by directors may only be conducted in a registered offering or under an available exemption from registration. The principal exemption available for directors is Securities Act Rule 144, which permits the public sale of limited amounts of securities without registration in ordinary brokers' transactions. Rule 144 has special filing and disclosure requirements, including a requirement to file a Form 144 at the time of or before the execution of any sale transaction. The safe harbor for sales under Rule 144 applies for 90 days after a director leaves office. It is important, therefore, for directors to consult with legal counsel or qualified compliance personnel before engaging in any sales of the corporation's securities, even after leaving office.

3. Insider Ownership and Short-Swing Profits (Section 16)

Section 16 of the Securities Exchange Act of 1934 and related SEC rules require specified insiders—directors, executive officers, and more than

10 percent shareholders—of public companies to report all of their holdings of and transactions in the corporation's equity securities. Any person who becomes an insider must file a report of beneficial ownership (i.e., pecuniary interest) within 10 days after becoming an insider. Thereafter, the insider must generally file reports whenever there is a change in ownership within two business days after such change. The names of any insiders who are delinquent in their filings must be disclosed in the corporation's annual meeting proxy statement. Delinquencies can also trigger monetary fines. Beneficial ownership includes not only the insider's direct ownership but also securities owned by the insider's spouse, dependents living at the insider's home, and trusts or entities under the insider's control. The rules also apply to derivative securities (i.e., securities that derive their value from the value of the corporation's equity securities), such as stock options.

Section 16(b) also requires insiders to disgorge to the corporation any profit from purchases and sales of the corporation's equity securities within a six-month period (subject to limited exceptions). This "short-swing profit" is measured as the difference between the highest sales price and the lowest purchase price of the securities within the six-month period. The requirement applies whether or not the insider had inside information at the time of the transactions. It also applies for the six months following a director's departure from the board. Importantly, these laws are enforced by an aggressive plaintiffs' bar that monitors SEC filings and brings claims against insiders "on behalf" of the corporation.

The SEC has adopted rules that provide exemptions from short-swing liability for transactions under employee benefit plans, transactions with the corporation (e.g., option grants), and gifts and inheritances, to cite a few. These regulations and exemptions are highly technical and can apply even after one ceases to be an insider. Insiders should consult with legal counsel familiar with these rules before committing to a transaction in the corporation's securities or derivative securities.

E. FAIR DISCLOSURE

The SEC's Regulation FD (for "fair disclosure") provides that a public company and its agents may not selectively disclose material information about the corporation to market participants, such as analysts, brokers, investment advisors, and shareholders who may act on the information before this information is made generally available. Rather, the corporation must take steps to disseminate such information in a manner that makes it broadly available to all market participants simultaneously. As a result, directors should be careful not to violate Regulation FD by disclosing material non-public information about the corporation. In particular, if a director engages directly with investors or market professionals, it is imperative to know what is and is not material non-public information. For this reason, it is helpful to have an investor relations or other executive officer present during these discussions to help the director navigate this area. Violations of Regulation FD have resulted in SEC enforcement actions and fines against public companies and individuals speaking on their behalf. Regulation FD has caused public companies to adopt policies that limit the persons authorized to speak on their behalf with securities analysts and other market participants.

F. COMPLIANCE PROGRAMS

Many public companies have established compliance programs, and have designated specific individuals, to assist directors in complying with their responsibilities under the federal securities laws. These programs are designed to ensure that the corporation makes complete, accurate, and timely disclosure of material information as required by SEC rules, complies with securities registration requirements, and satisfies other securities law obligations. In addition, these programs help directors and other insiders to comply with insider trading and other applicable laws and help the corporation to meet its obligations under Regulation FD to avoid improper selective disclosure. Directors of public companies should be familiar with their and the corporation's responsibilities and seek the advice of counsel whenever questions arise.

CHAPTER

6 Mergers and Acquisitions and Defensive Actions

Merger and acquisition (M&A) transactions, as well as contests for corporate control, are extraordinary situations that are among the most demanding that directors encounter. Decisions implicating control of the corporation present a greater potential for director conflicts of interest than ordinary business decisions. As a result, many states apply different legal standards to director actions relating to these transactions than those that apply to ordinary business decisions.

The following is an overview of the fiduciary principles applicable to director decisions in the M&A context. The legal standards described are based principally on Delaware law as interpreted by the Delaware courts, because Delaware has the most well-developed body of law on the topic. Although many courts outside of Delaware often consider Delaware legal standards when ruling on challenges to director conduct, Delaware legal standards are not binding on other states, and some states have expressly chosen not to apply Delaware legal standards.

A. DUTIES OF DIRECTORS WHEN A SALE TRANSACTION DOES NOT INVOLVE A SALE OF CONTROL

When a company is sold, different duties may apply depending on whether courts view the transaction as a "sale of control." A cash sale of a company is deemed a sale of control, but a stock-for-stock sale may not be. Delaware courts generally view stock-for-stock sales as not involving a sale of control where there will be no controlling shareholder following the transaction, because shareholders retain the possibility of receiving a control premium in the future. Whether a sale for a combination of cash and stock constitutes a sale of control depends on the circumstances, including the percentage of the total consideration represented by cash (e.g., a half-cash/half-stock transaction has been deemed to be a sale of control).

Courts review stock-for-stock transactions that do not involve a sale of control under the business judgment rule, which is the standard of review that is most deferential to directors' judgment and the one that applies to most decisions. As such, directors have broad latitude to select the transaction they believe provides the corporation and its shareholders the best long-term prospects for growth and value enhancement, without the need to maximize short-term return. Moreover, directors can consider matters such as the location of the combined company's headquarters, who will be CEO of the combined company, and the composition of the combined company's board.

B. DUTIES OF DIRECTORS IN SALE OF CONTROL TRANSACTIONS

If a target board engages in a transaction that will result in a sale of control, the directors will generally bear the burden of showing that they undertook a reasonable process directed to attaining the highest value reasonably available for the corporation's shareholders. This standard, which was first articulated by the Delaware Supreme Court in a case involving Revlon, Inc., is often referred to as the *Revlon* standard and is an "intermediate" standard of review, between the more deferential business judgment rule discussed above and the more stringent "entire fairness" standard discussed below. Courts reviewing whether directors have complied with this standard consider both the adequacy of the directors' decision-making process and the reasonableness of their decisions in light of the circumstances presented. Directors have the burden of showing that they were not conflicted, were adequately informed, and acted reasonably. There is no single blueprint for a board to fulfill its fiduciary duties, and directors may select among reasonable alternatives.

1. Conflicts of Interest

In reviewing whether the directors have satisfied their duties in connection with a sale of control, courts will consider whether any of the directors, management, or the directors' advisors had conflicts of interest in the transaction and, if so, whether those conflicts affected the sale process. Sale transactions that present actual or potential conflicts of interest include:

- transactions in which directors or officers will remain owners of the corporation after the transaction is completed (other than on a pro rata basis no different than other shareholders); and
- transactions in which directors or officers receive, or are affiliated with shareholders who receive, benefits not shared by all shareholders.

In transactions in which some directors or officers have an actual or potential conflict, the non-conflicted directors should structure and manage the sale process to protect against claims that the process was affected by the participation of the conflicted directors or officers. In many cases where directors have an actual or potential conflict, those directors are recused from the sale process. Recusal may be accomplished by the involved directors agreeing to recuse themselves from the sale process or by the board forming a committee of non-conflicted directors to oversee the sale process. In the event of a management conflict, directors need to assert more direct control and take care to ensure that the member(s) of management in question are properly recused from negotiations and decision making that can be impacted by their conflict.

In addition, directors should determine whether the financial and legal advisors engaged to assist the corporation in connection with the transaction have any potential conflicts of interest that could affect the sale process. Advisor conflicts may arise from, for example, relationships with parties on the other side of the transaction, such as representation of a buyer in prior recent transactions or the receipt of significant advisor fees from the buyer in recent years. Directors should ask their advisors about relationships or other matters that may present potential conflicts not only at the outset of the advisors' engagement but also to the extent new parties emerge during the sale process. When actual or potential conflicts exist or arise, the board may choose a different advisor or, in appropriate circumstances, ensure that the advisors take steps to reduce the impact of the actual or potential conflict on the sale process. Directors should also actively monitor the sale process to make sure that it is not affected by the conflict. In some circumstances, directors may want to consider hiring a financial advisor without conflicts in addition to the conflicted financial advisor.

2. Complying with *Revlon* "Sale of Control" Duties

The *Revlon* standard does not mandate any specific sale process, such as a pre-signing auction, and directors are not guarantors that the best price has been obtained. Directors have substantial discretion to follow any sale process they reasonably believe is likely to produce the most favorable transaction for the shareholders. In general, courts have recognized that the business judgment rule protects a disinterested board's determination as to how to conduct a sale process. Even in a sale of control, a board may reasonably determine to enter into a merger agreement following arm's-length negotiation with one bidder, as opposed to conducting an auction or canvassing the market, if the board determines in good faith that such approach is more favorable, so long as the agreement does not preclude the board from considering other bidders who may present a "topping" bid after the original deal is announced.

In Delaware, under *Revlon*, when a board is choosing between two cash bids that are comparable in terms of timing and likelihood of consummation, the board is required to look only to price and cannot, for example, take a lower bid because it is better for employees, customers, suppliers, the community, or other non-shareholder constituencies. State law does, however, vary with respect to the extent to which directors may consider the interests of non-shareholder constituencies in choosing between alternative transactions. In some states, interests of non-shareholder constituencies may be considered only to the extent they are consistent with shareholder interests. In other states, however, the interests of non-shareholder constituencies are permitted or required to be considered separately from shareholder interests.

When choosing among multiple offers, *Revlon* does not require the board to simply accept the highest nominal price. Directors may discount the nominal price by financing, regulatory, and other factors that impact the likelihood that an offer will result in a completed transaction. Accordingly, a board may conclude that an offer with substantial likelihood of consummation may be superior to a higher offer that has significant financing, regulatory, or other risks to consummation.

A court considering compliance with the *Revlon* standard will not second-guess a choice from among several reasonable alternatives, provided that the sale process was not tainted by conflicts of interest and the directors had a reasonable, informed basis for believing the alternative they chose would produce the best result for shareholders. This would be the case even if the court might have decided differently or later events prove the decision wrong.

Moreover, in Delaware, if the sale transaction not involving a controlling shareholder is approved by a fully informed and non-coerced vote of the holders of a majority of the disinterested shares, the *Revlon* standard would no longer apply and the business judgment rule would become the applicable standard of review by the court in any post-closing lawsuit for damages.

C. CONTROLLING SHAREHOLDER TRANSACTIONS

Certain types of transactions are subject to the "entire fairness" standard, the most stringent standard of review applied by courts to sale transactions. For example, the entire fairness standard applies to sale transactions in which a controlling shareholder is part of the buyer group or is being treated differently from other shareholders. The entire fairness standard also applies when:

- a majority of the selling corporation's directors have business, financial, or other material relationships with the buyer or an interest different from other shareholders; or
- a majority of the selling corporation's directors lack independence from or are dominated by the buyer.

If the controlling shareholder is selling to a third party in a sale transaction and is receiving the same consideration as other shareholders, there is normally no conflict between the interests of the controlling shareholder and those of the minority shareholders. Thus, the entire fairness standard would normally not apply.

Courts do not apply a bright-line test to assess whether an individual director is conflicted or whether a shareholder is a controlling shareholder for purposes of assessing whether the entire fairness standard will apply. However, conflicts generally must be material to be considered disabling. A controlling shareholder, moreover, need not control a majority of the company's voting stock to be deemed controlling if the controlling shareholder exercises a combination of voting power and management control such that it has effective control of the board.

Courts view controlling shareholder transactions as presenting an inherent conflict between the personal interests of the conflicted directors or the controlling shareholder and their fiduciary duties to the other shareholders. As a result, the normal presumptions that attach to business decisions made by disinterested directors do not apply, and the controlling shareholder and/or conflicted directors must demonstrate the "entire fairness" of the transaction's terms. The entire fairness standard considers both the fairness of the price paid in the transaction and the process by which the transaction was conducted.

A conflicted transaction with a controlling shareholder may, however, avoid application of the entire fairness standard and be considered under the more lenient business judgment rule if:

- the controlling shareholder conditions the possible transaction, at the outset, on approval by both a special committee of disinterested directors and the holders of a majority of the shares not held by the controlling shareholder and its affiliates or the corporation's executive officers (sometimes known as approval by a "majority of the minority");
- the special committee is independent, discharges its duty of care, is able to choose its own advisors, and is empowered to be able to say "no"; and
- the disinterested shareholder vote is fully informed and not coerced.

By contrast, where a conflicted controlling shareholder transaction is conditioned at the outset upon approval by *either* a special committee of disinterested directors *or* a majority of the unaffiliated shareholders, *but not both*, the transaction will continue to be subject to the more stringent entire fairness review (with the modest litigation benefit of shifting the burden to the plaintiff), rather than business judgment review.

D. DUTIES OF DIRECTORS CONSIDERING AN UNSOLICITED ACQUISITION PROPOSAL

Upon receipt of a credible unsolicited acquisition proposal, directors should review the proposal and determine whether pursuing it is in the best interests of the corporation and its shareholders. Directors are not obligated to accept an unsolicited offer, negotiate or enter into discussions with an offeror, abandon the corporation's long-term strategy, or sell the corporation, even if the proposal offers a substantial premium to the current market price of the corporation's stock. In determining whether to pursue the proposal, the directors may consider the opportunities and risks of continuing to run the business over the short, medium, and long terms. The board generally will engage a financial advisor to assist it in evaluating the financial aspects of the unsolicited proposal in comparison to continuing with the corporation's long-term strategy and outside legal counsel to assist directors in understanding their legal obligations and fiduciary duties.

Unless the directors are conflicted or make no efforts to be adequately informed, the business judgment rule will apply to the decision of whether to pursue an unsolicited third-party acquisition proposal. Enhanced scrutiny will generally not apply to a board's refusal to engage in negotiations with an offeror (i.e., targets of unsolicited offers may "just say no"). The fact that the proposal may result in the directors not staying in office does not in itself create a conflict for the directors considering the proposal. If such a decision is challenged, the court will not second-guess judgments made by directors who have fulfilled their duties of care and loyalty.

As discussed below, however, if a board decides to take defensive measures against an unsolicited proposal, courts may apply more stringent standards to that decision.

E. DEFENSIVE ACTIONS

If directors take defensive action to potential threats to control, such as adopting a shareholder rights plan (also known as a "poison pill") in response to an unsolicited proposal or agree to deal protections in merger agreements (such as "no shop" provisions and termination fees, discussed below), the courts will apply an enhanced level of scrutiny known as the *Unocal* test, named after a landmark Delaware Supreme Court decision involving a hostile bid for Unocal Corporation. Under *Unocal* review, courts apply a two-pronged analysis that looks to whether there is a reasonably perceived threat to the corporation justifying a response, and whether the chosen response is reasonable in relation to the threat posed.

When the *Unocal* standard applies, directors may demonstrate that they had reasonable grounds to believe there was a threat to the corporation by showing that the board consisted of a majority of non-conflicted directors who relied on the advice of legal counsel and financial advisors. The reasonableness of the response is evaluated in the context of the specific threat. Often there will be more than one reasonable response and the board may choose any reasonable response, even if the court or shareholders might have made a different choice. If the directors show they had reasonable grounds to believe that a threat to the corporation existed and that the defensive action chosen was reasonable and proportionate, the business judgment rule applies to the defensive action.

The board's response is not reasonable if it is preclusive or coercive. A preclusive response effectively precludes other alternatives because it makes any alternative to the board's response mathematically impossible or realistically unattainable. A response is coercive if it effectively forces shareholders to accept a response that they have no real choice but to accept because of negative consequences to their investment.

In addition, courts will consider whether the response is proportionate to the threat. A response that has a limited duration and maintains the flexibility of the board to address future events is generally viewed as reasonable and proportionate. For example, courts have viewed as a reasonable and proportionate defensive response a poison pill that stays in place for a finite period of time and that can be redeemed or amended by a future board. In contrast, a poison pill that can be redeemed or amended only by the current board, and not by future directors, has been found to be an unreasonable and disproportionate response because it prevents shareholders from electing other directors who would redeem or otherwise terminate the poison pill.

Defensive actions related to shareholder voting are viewed by Delaware courts with special concern and subject to a more stringent review. In such instances, courts generally apply the *Unocal* standard with a sensitivity to the shareholder franchise. Although directors may use corporate funds to solicit shareholders to vote as the directors recommend and may delay a meeting for a short period of time to provide shareholders with updated information material to the matter, the possibility that one or more directors would lose the election if the vote were held as scheduled will not by itself be a sufficient justification to delay, postpone, or cancel a meeting. By contrast, in votes on sale transactions where directors do not have a conflicting interest, directors have successfully demonstrated that sufficient justification exists to postpone a vote in instances where they credibly demonstrate that they are doing so not to perpetuate their control of the corporation but to preserve for shareholders what they reasonably believe to be a value-maximizing opportunity.

F. PROTECTING AN APPROVED TRANSACTION

The board's duties do not end with the signing of a merger or sale agreement. Until shareholders approve the agreement, directors must consider any superior proposals and other developments that affect the directors' initial recommendation that shareholders vote in favor of the transaction.

Many merger or sale agreements contain so-called "deal protection" provisions, which are subject to the *Unocal* standard for defensive actions described above. Deal protection provisions limit the right of the directors to solicit alternative proposals, respond to competing proposals, or change their recommendation that shareholders vote in favor of the transaction. Courts have generally found deal protection provisions to be consistent with the *Unocal* standard so long as they are reasonable. In the merger context, merger agreements should allow the target's directors to consider post-signing developments that occur prior to the shareholder vote and make accurate disclosure to shareholders regarding the board's recommendation of the original transaction.

One important category of deal protections contained in many merger agreements is a provision requiring that a termination fee be paid to the buyer if the board changes its recommendation to shareholders or terminates the agreement in order to accept a superior transaction. The purpose of this fee is to compensate the buyer for its time and effort in reaching the original agreement and effectively set a floor for a potential superior transaction. Although Delaware courts have cautioned that each termination fee must be tested in the context of the specific transaction, they have routinely found that termination fees in the range of three to four percent of the equity value of the transaction meet the *Unocal* standard.

Part III:
Board and Committee Structure and Process

CHAPTER

7 Overview of Board Structure and Process

Effective board structures and processes are critical to the board's ability to discharge its responsibilities. Most boards meet at scheduled times and base their deliberations on information provided to them by management. Apart from their board service, most independent directors have limited relationships with the corporation that would provide any additional insights on the corporation. Board structure and process (including information flow to the board) help to mitigate the limitations of time constraints and information asymmetry. They are critical to enabling directors to satisfy their duties and allow them to form objective viewpoints about the issues facing the corporation and the quality of the management team.

No single governance model fits every corporation. Instead, each board should tailor its approach to the corporation's unique needs and circumstances. The objective is to establish a culture of discipline, objectivity, and efficiency to inform the work of the board.

A. BOARD COMPOSITION

1. Board Size

Board size varies significantly from one corporation to the next, with nine to 12 being a common range for larger public companies. Assembling the skills necessary for the board and its committees to discharge their responsibilities effectively is a key matter. Board size may also be influenced by independence and other regulatory requirements, relationships with significant shareholders and other stakeholders, cost, diversity objectives, and scheduling practicalities. Each board should evaluate the appropriate board size on a regular basis.

2. Nomination Process

Directors have considerable influence over the composition of the board. They are responsible for nominating (and re-nominating) candidates for election by shareholders and for filling board vacancies between shareholder meetings. Public company boards need to explain why each candidate for election by shareholders is suitably qualified, and boards should revisit, on an annual basis, the "fit" and contribution of each nominee, in light of the corporation's strategic direction, the board's needs, and each nominee's contribution. The nominating and governance committee is typically responsible for identifying and recommending to the board the mix of expertise, experience, and independence on the board to serve the corporation's present and future needs. This recommendation is often based on a list of personal qualities required of individual directors as well as a matrix or list of skill sets and qualifications desired of directors. It is good practice for these tools to be updated periodically.

3. Considerations for Director Candidates

Directors must devote substantial time and attention to discharge their responsibilities effectively. The time required will vary considerably depending on the corporation's size, complexity, stage of maturity, and the matters at hand. Time required includes the time directors spend on meeting preparation and attendance, informal consultations with other board members and management, and ongoing review of materials to keep up with changing developments. Committee work puts additional demands on directors, particularly when they sit on the audit or compensation committee. When the organization faces special situations, such as change-of-control transactions, shareholder activism, transactions with controlling shareholders, financial distress situations, compliance issues, financial restatements, and management succession issues, even more will be demanded from some or all of the directors.

Directors considering new or continued board service must understand the scope of the job (recognizing that the scope may change significantly depending on the circumstances) and weigh carefully the time required to satisfy their responsibilities. The board must consider a board candidate's ability to devote the necessary time to be an effective director before nominating or re-nominating the individual. Because of proxy advisory firm positions, many boards of public companies establish limits on the number of other boards on which a director may serve and also require that directors inform the board before accepting additional board service or other significant commitments.

B. BOARD OBJECTIVITY AND DIRECTOR INDEPENDENCE

Directors must form their own judgments about what is in the best interests of the corporation and its shareholders. This obligation extends to assessments of management's performance and the strategies proposed by management. Objectivity and independence require constructive skepticism concerning management proposals and the willingness to challenge management, including, for example, by testing management's assumptions.

1. Independence

Independence is an important theme in corporate governance. The U.S. stock exchanges require listed companies to have a majority of "independent" directors, as defined by the applicable exchange. These exchanges also require that key oversight committees—audit, compensation, and, in the case of the NYSE, nominating and governance—be composed solely of independent directors.

Generally, the U.S. stock exchanges provide that a director is independent only if the board makes an affirmative determination that the director is free of any material family, charitable, business, or professional relationship (other than stock ownership and the directorship) with the corporation, its management, or its auditors that is reasonably likely to affect the director's objectivity. In addition, audit and compensation committee members must meet separate definitions of independence under federal securities laws. These definitions are more stringent than U.S. stock exchange definitions of director independence.

When making annual independence determinations, the board should consider all relevant facts and circumstances, and it should review the materiality of a director's relationships, both to the director and to the organization or person with whom the director has a relationship. For public companies, the names of the independent directors must be disclosed in the corporation's proxy statement along with the principles underlying the independence determination, as well as any transactions, relationships, or arrangements the board considered in the independence determination but were not otherwise disclosed. U.S. stock exchange listing standards also identify certain relationships deemed as always inconsistent with a finding of independence.

Even if a director is independent under U.S. stock exchange definitions, the director will not necessarily be considered independent and disinterested with respect to all board decisions. In reviewing director actions in a particular conflict of interest situation or in a special committee context, courts will evaluate the range of business, social, and personal relationships among the directors participating in the decision or transaction, on the one hand, and the corporation, any controlling shareholders, members of senior management, or other relevant parties, on the other hand.

2. Executive Sessions

Executive sessions of independent directors without management present have become a common practice. These sessions provide a forum for non-management and independent directors to raise matters, such as CEO performance or succession issues, that they might otherwise be reluctant to raise with management present. Many boards and board committees hold an executive session at each regular meeting. U.S. stock exchanges require periodic executive sessions.

If the CEO is also the board chair, a lead independent director convenes and presides at executive sessions. Although an agenda may be prepared for an executive session, it is also common for the session to be open-ended, allowing non-management and independent directors to discuss any matters related to the corporation or its management. To facilitate open and candid discussions regarding sensitive issues, detailed minutes of executive sessions are not typically kept. It is important, however, to record attendance and any major decisions made as well as communicate to management any substantive information from executive sessions of which management should be aware.

C. BOARD LEADERSHIP

Historically, CEOs of public companies have often served as board chairs. In response to pressure from institutional investors and proxy advisory firms, many public companies now separate the two functions with the chair position being held by an independent director who provides leadership to the board. Each board should decide what is the most appropriate model for its corporate environment and culture. Public companies must disclose their board leadership structure, the rationale for that structure, and its relationship to risk oversight.

Where the CEO or another non-independent director serves as board chair, the independent directors often formally designate an independent director to act as a "lead" director. An independent board chair or lead director can be a helpful counterweight to and business partner of a combined board chair and CEO. The existence of an independent board chair or lead director should not inhibit the ability of other directors to communicate directly with the CEO.

The independent board chair or lead director typically works with the CEO to prepare the board agenda and determine the types of information to be distributed to the board and its committees, presides at executive sessions of the non-management directors, and serves as the board's liaison to the CEO between meetings. Importantly, the lead independent director can ensure that there is an appropriate flow of information to all board members. The independent board chair or lead director may also be called upon by the board to meet with shareholders. The NYSE requires listed companies to identify publicly, by name or position, the director or directors who preside at meetings of non-management directors and to inform shareholders and other interested parties how to communicate with non-management directors.

D. BOARD DECISION MAKING

1. How Board Action Is Taken

Directors exercise their authority in a variety of ways. They oversee the operation of the organization's business and give direction to management. They are also responsible for making specific decisions, such as hiring and firing the CEO and approving major transactions.

Formal adoption of resolutions is sometimes, but not always, necessary for board or committee actions. Some actions may simply result from a consensus or a "sense of the board." As a matter of law, some actions (e.g., changes in the articles or certificate of incorporation, authorization of dividends or stock repurchases, issuance of shares, election of officers, and the approval of mergers, financings, or corporate liquidations) require formal board action (as well as shareholder action, in some cases). Directors may take formal action only at a duly held meeting of the board or board committee or by unanimous written consent. Generally, because they do not allow for discussion among directors, unanimous written consents are advisable only for routine matters or matters on which consensus has been reached in a recent meeting of the board or committee. Unlike shareholders, directors may not act by proxy; directors must be present at a meeting to act at the meeting.

Unexpected events or corporate crises may prompt important corporate decisions to be made at quickly convened special board meetings. A well-developed crisis plan and familiarity with the corporation can streamline decision making under these circumstances. Nevertheless, meeting minutes should adequately memorialize these instances.

2. Information

The quality of the information available to directors significantly affects their effectiveness. Management should aim to provide the board with information that is:

- timely and relevant;
- concise, fair, and accurate;
- well-organized;
- supported by background or historical data necessary to place the information in context; and
- designed to inform directors of all material aspects of the corporation's business, performance, and prospects, including major challenges, and allow them to exercise effectively their objective decision making.

Directors should receive information sufficiently in advance of board or committee meetings to allow careful study and thoughtful reflection, and to accommodate requests for additional information.

To assist in their oversight role, directors have access to employees and management. At many corporations, directors communicate directly with senior-level employees to learn more about the corporation's business. Some corporations schedule site visits for non-management directors so they can observe business operations and speak with employees at the operating level of the business.

Boards may rely on information provided by employees, officers, and legal counsel so long as such reliance is reasonable, and boards may also consult other outside advisors. The need for and extent of consultation with outside advisors varies among companies and industries as well as the matter under consideration. For example, boards involved in discussions about a merger or material acquisition often engage investment bankers for advice. Boards of companies in industries with significant environmental, health, safety, or other regulatory risks may choose to engage outside consultants to review the corporation's policies and procedures regarding such risks. Many board compensation committees employ an independent compensation consultant. The use of compensation consultants is covered in more detail in Chapter 9.

3. Disagreements and Resignations

Boards usually make decisions by consensus. However, acting in the best interests of the corporation and its shareholders does not always require unanimous agreement. If, after a thorough discussion, a director disagrees with any significant action the board is taking, the director can consider voting against the proposal. If the director does vote against or abstain from voting on a proposal, the director should ensure that the vote against or the abstention is recorded in the minutes of the meeting.

Except in extreme circumstances, taking a dissenting position need not cause a director to consider resigning. Although resignation is a fact-dependent decision, some factors that can cause a director to consider resignation include the following:

- management or the board is acting inappropriately;
- management is not dealing in good faith with the directors;
- management or the board is not dealing in good faith with shareholders or the public; or
- the information being disclosed by the corporation is inadequate, incorrect, or misleading and the director is unable to convince the board to take appropriate action.

A director may also consider resigning if the director's point of view is being regularly and intentionally disregarded. Public companies are required to disclose a director's resignation, and in some cases the reason for the resignation, in an SEC filing.

E. BOARD MEETINGS

1. Number of Meetings and Scheduling of Meetings

The number of regular board meetings will vary with the size, complexity, and culture of the corporation as well as the corporation's circumstances. Some boards prefer frequent, short meetings, whereas others prefer fewer, lengthier meetings. Some boards schedule one extended planning or strategic meeting each year and shorter meetings during the rest of the year.

Boards typically should hold regularly scheduled meetings at least quarterly. Many boards schedule six to eight regular meetings per year and hold additional special meetings as needed, particularly if a crisis occurs.

The necessary time allotted to board and committee meetings requires careful planning. Meetings should balance management presentations with discussion among directors and with management. Appropriate reports and analyses furnished in advance facilitate discussion at the meeting.

2. Agenda

The board's agenda determines the matters that come before the board at any meeting and therefore where the board focuses its attention. Due to management's greater knowledge of the day-to-day operations and immediate needs of the corporation, the CEO and senior managers often play a significant role in determining the matters to be presented to the board. For the board to be effective and objective, however, it must play an active role in setting its own agenda. Thus, the trend is toward increasing independent director involvement in determining the board agenda via the independent board chair or lead director. All directors should have the opportunity to request that an item be included on the agenda.

The board and the corporate secretary or other support staff should prepare an annual agenda of key items requiring recurring and focused attention by the board and each committee, such as progress against (as well as periodic re-examination and updating of) operational and financial plans, evaluation of the CEO, and other executive management performance. The annual agenda should also include the evaluation of board and committee performance as well as the effectiveness of internal controls and procedures designed to address legal compliance, risk management, corporate policy adherence, and accounting and financial reporting.

3. Minutes

Meetings of the board of directors and board committees should be reflected in minutes prepared and circulated promptly by the corporate secretary or another person skilled in preparing minutes. The board or committee should carefully review the minutes, which are generally prepared in draft form by the general counsel or corporate secretary, and consider them for amendment or approval, typically at the next meeting of the board or committee. Board minutes are the official record of meetings and important legal documents that may be reviewed by professionals such as the corporation's auditors, lending banks and underwriters, claimants against the corporation or its directors or officers, and reviewing courts.

Although there are differing opinions among corporate advisors about the appropriate level of detail, minutes should be sufficient to support the availability of the applicable protections provided to directors by substantive law. Generally, minutes should summarize important discussions and actions, without purporting to provide a verbatim record. Minutes that do not reflect an adequate deliberative process may support an inference that directors failed to consider pertinent information fully, to deliberate with due care, or, in certain cases, to act with loyalty to the corporation.

Well-drafted minutes can be helpful in litigation. If named as defendants or called as witnesses, directors may be required to explain their actions well after the fact. Appropriately detailed minutes may provide a contemporaneous record of their deliberative process and can help when the adequacy of that process is challenged.

Directors should request confirmation that the corporation maintains permanent records containing copies of the information provided to the board, such as board books and management or other presentations. This information can help demonstrate the board's informed business judgment and assist directors in accurately recollecting past events. The corporation should develop, with board approval, a consistent policy for the retention and security of such information so that, together with quality minutes, there is a reliable record of the board's deliberations.

4. Notes

Note taking presents discrete issues to be carefully considered. Directors are not obligated to take notes. Those directors who take notes to help them participate should consider whether to retain them. Unlike the process related to board or committee minutes, notes are not subject to a careful process of drafting, review, or approval, and they may contain statements or notations that can be misinterpreted, taken out of context, or incorrect. To avoid possible dissonance and confusion, many companies encourage that all notes and draft minutes be discarded after approval of the official minutes.

5. Discussions Outside the Boardroom

Individual directors often discuss the corporation and its business with management or with one another outside of board meetings. One-on-one discussions can efficiently tap into a director's expertise or point of view and yield a "sense of the board" when formal action is not required. Indeed, these discussions are inevitable and generally may be beneficial to the corporation.

On the other hand, care should be taken when regular communications outside the board and committee rooms, particularly between management and a select group of directors, could lead to uneven knowledge among directors about important corporate matters. They may also impair the collective, inclusive, and candid exchange of views at board or committee meetings and interfere with the board's collegial and independent relationship with management. Moreover, because official action by directors can occur only at a duly called meeting at which a quorum is present or by unanimous written consent, individual "polling" of directors is not effective to authorize action requiring board approval.

F. DELEGATION TO COMMITTEES

The laws of most states permit the board of directors to delegate authority to committees of directors. With some exceptions, boards can delegate as much or as little authority to their committees as they consider appropriate. Public company boards are required to delegate certain responsibilities to committees, such as designing and approving executive compensation and oversight of the corporation's financial reporting process and internal controls. Even when a corporation chooses to or is required to delegate certain actions to a committee, U.S. stock exchange listing standards and applicable state law specify actions only the full board can take, such as approving the corporation's annual financial statements or any proposed amendments to the corporation's articles or certificate of incorporation.

Each board should tailor its processes and committee structure to the corporation's specific circumstances, including its size, the complexity of its operations and risk management issues, the regulatory requirements applicable to its operations, and the competitive environment in which it operates. Further, the board or an appropriate committee of the board, such as the nominating and governance committee, should periodically review the responsibilities assigned to each committee and consider whether the assignments of duties and responsibilities continue to be appropriate and consistent with the corporation's needs and objectives.

1. Determining the Right Committee Scope

Practice varies with respect to how board committees function. Some boards do most of their work through committees, reserving to the full board only the highest-level strategy and policy matters and those legally required to be addressed by the board. Others delegate to committees only to the extent required.

2. Determining the Right Committee Structure

Practice also varies with respect to committee structure. Boards may delegate to a particular standing or special committee matters that require knowledge, experience, or a significant additional time commitment. Also, delegation of certain matters to committees of independent directors can help to neutralize potential conflicts of interest.

a. Required Committees

U.S. stock exchange listing standards or federal securities laws generally require audit and compensation committees to be composed exclusively of independent directors. In addition, the NYSE listing standards require corporations to have a nominating and governance committee composed exclusively of independent directors. Regulators in some industries may require or encourage boards to establish committees to address specific issues (such as the oversight of risk in some financial institutions).

b. Other Standing Committees

In addition to the committees mandated by federal law and U.S. stock exchange listing standards, a board may establish other standing committees to oversee ongoing matters, such as risk management, safety, environmental issues, technology, or public policy. Key factors to consider in creating a standing committee include:

- whether it is more efficient and effective for a subset of the full board to develop an understanding of the relevant topic and to use that expertise to review and monitor the issues in that area;
- whether it is more efficient and effective for an existing standing committee to oversee particular matters, rather than create a new committee; and
- in the case of public company boards, the disclosure implications of creating additional standing committees and compensating directors for service on those committees.

With the increased emphasis on the role played by independent directors, the practice of appointing executive committees composed of management directors and other directors who are available to meet on short notice to address matters between regular meetings of the board has waned.

c. Special Committees

From time to time, a board may establish a special committee to undertake a specific project or responsibility. In those instances, defining the scope of delegated authority and responsibility of the committee is important. For example, a board may decide to form a special committee of disinterested directors to consider transactions involving conflicts of interest between the corporation and its officers. The members of this type of special committee should be disinterested in the subject matter and otherwise able to exercise independent judgment. The committee should also establish procedures for its deliberations and its powers, including the ability to hire independent advisors. A properly constituted and operating special committee of independent directors may reduce the risk of a successful challenge to the board's actions and the potential for director liability. A board may also form what are sometimes called "committees of convenience," which are committees that are not driven by any concern of conflicts but are created to facilitate the workings of the board on a topic. For example, some boards engaged in an M&A situation, whether a transaction or a consideration of strategic alternatives, might form a "transaction committee" or a "strategic review committee," in which a subset of directors (usually with some expertise in the matter at hand) will meet more frequently, together with advisors, in between meetings of the full board.

A public company board may also form a special committee of independent, disinterested directors to conduct investigations involving potential litigation or wrongdoing. In these cases, the board usually authorizes the committee to engage independent legal counsel and other advisors to help the committee investigate the facts and determine appropriate action. The exact scope of authority and functions of the committee will depend on the unique circumstances of the committee's charge, including the credibility of the allegations, the nature of the alleged wrongdoing, and the familiarity of the committee members with the issues. Depending on the scope of authority delegated to the committee, the committee should complete the investigation and then take appropriate action on behalf of the board or recommend an appropriate course of action to the board of directors.

If allowed under state law and the corporation's organizational documents, a board occasionally may desire to create a single-person committee. For example, a board may need to react quickly to market conditions and delegate to a one-member committee the authority to price a securities offering within parameters previously established by the board. Other than in that kind of limited context, single-person committees are generally not ideal because courts may view such committees as reflecting a less robust process and consequently apply a higher level of scrutiny to any action taken by such committees.

3. Duties of Committee Members and Board Oversight of Committees

Directors serving on board committees are subject to the same duties of care and loyalty and are entitled to the same protections as they are when acting as members of the board. Delegation of a given responsibility to a committee does not relieve the board of ultimate responsibility for oversight of the corporation. Directors may, however, rely in good faith upon the efforts and reports of the committees to which they delegate matters. At the same time, in accordance with their obligation to provide oversight, boards should ensure that committees establish appropriate procedures, including keeping minutes and records and providing a regular flow of reports and information to the board to ensure that all directors are kept abreast of each committee's activities and significant decisions. Generally, standing committees should provide reports at regularly scheduled board meetings and make available to all directors committee agendas, minutes, and written reports.

G. COMMITTEE RESPONSIBILITIES AND COMPOSITION

To the extent not dictated by federal regulations and U.S. stock exchange listing standards, committee responsibilities and composition vary from corporation to corporation. Below are general guidelines for each area.

1. Committee Responsibilities

Each committee's scope of responsibility should be tailored to the matters being delegated to that committee. Delegation to a committee may be accomplished pursuant to the corporation's bylaws or through board resolutions or a formal committee charter, though typically committee charters are used for standing committees. The board should give due consideration to defining the scope of the committee's responsibilities and authority, including:

- defining the subjects the committee should address;
- determining the committee's scope and limits of authority (e.g., whether the committee is empowered to act on behalf of the board or whether the committee is to recommend action to the board);

- ensuring appropriate independence, including the authority to engage independent legal counsel and other advisors at the corporation's expense;
- establishing standards for committee engagement, including frequency of meetings;
- ensuring regular reporting to the board (except in the case of certain special committees); and
- determining whether a committee should be a standing or a special committee.

2. Committee Composition

The board should select committee members using criteria appropriate to the committee's purpose and in compliance with any applicable laws and U.S. stock exchange listing standards. Under most state statutes, each member of a board committee must be a duly elected or appointed member of the board of directors. Committee membership criteria may include:

- experience relevant to committee responsibilities;
- subject matter expertise that will assist the committee in its work;
- ability to meet requisite time commitments;
- disinterest in the committee's subject matter; and
- independence from management.

Other considerations may include refreshment and diversity.

H. ADVISORS

Boards generally look to the corporation's general counsel as the primary resource for legal and governance advice. The general counsel's client is the corporation, as represented by the board of directors, not the CEO or any other officer or employee. For this reason, many boards and key board committees meet regularly in a private session with the general counsel. In addition, the board and each of its committees should have access to the corporation's regular outside counsel, if there is one, and should have the authority and reasonable funding to retain legal counsel and professional advisors of the board's or committee's choosing. A specific circumstance (e.g., allegations of management wrongdoing, negotiating executive pay packages, or a shareholder demand to bring a derivative suit) may prompt the board or, more likely, a board committee, to seek independent legal advice. More rarely, a board committee may also choose to have its own counsel, separate from the corporation's in-house and outside counsel, to advise the committee on a regular basis as to its duties and responsibilities.

The board and each of its committees should consider whether each is receiving appropriate advice regarding legal and compliance requirements and timely updates on legal risks. In addition, each committee should consider whether it has a good understanding of when to seek advice from lawyers or other external experts, in addition to the availability of advice from the corporation's general counsel and other internal resources.

I. BOARD AND COMMITTEE EVALUATIONS

Many boards evaluate their effectiveness and that of each of their committees on a regular basis. The U.S. stock exchanges require boards to engage in this process at least annually. While practice varies as to whether this process includes individual director evaluations, many corporations are including this type of assessment to promote continuous improvement and to ensure alignment with the corporation's strategy. Individual director assessments also demonstrate to shareholders the board's commitment to holding directors accountable for their performance.

Board and board committee self-evaluations are most effective when planned in advance, with participants understanding the purpose of the process and the topics to be addressed. The typical goals are to assess the board's fulfillment of its duties and responsibilities and consider ways in which the board and its committees can improve their processes. Many boards find formal or informal director interviews to be a helpful way for collecting input from individual directors for board and committee discussions. Other boards use written questionnaires to gather information. Questions on these forms should be drafted with care. Qualified external facilitators may be helpful in collecting information and presenting it in a manner that ensures that the views of individual directors remain confidential. Some boards also use external facilitators to lead discussions and provide an independent perspective. It may be useful to maintain in the minutes a record of the process followed and any specific decisions of the board or any committee that resulted, but often it is not necessary or appropriate to retain written materials collected as part of the process.

The nominating and governance committee generally oversees the board evaluation process, as discussed in Chapter 10.

CHAPTER

8 Audit Committee

The audit committee is critical to a corporation's corporate governance structure. In fact, its existence and some of its functions are legally mandated for public companies. It has primary responsibility for the board's oversight of the corporation's financial reporting process and internal controls. For public companies, it also has the exclusive responsibility for retaining and overseeing the performance, independence, and compensation of the corporation's external auditor. The audit committee serves as the board body to which internal and external auditors, as well as the corporation's legal counsel and senior financial compliance and ethics managers, may report and discuss issues relating to accounting, auditing, financial reporting, risk management, legal, compliance, and ethical matters.

A. MEMBERSHIP

Public company audit committees must consist solely of directors who satisfy independence requirements set forth in U.S. stock exchange listing standards and the federal securities laws. Audit committee members may not be affiliates of the corporation (i.e., they may not directly or indirectly control, be controlled by, or be under common control with the corporation or any of its subsidiaries (other than in their capacity as a member of the corporation's board or audit committee), where "control" means having the direct or indirect power to direct the management and policies of the entity). Audit committee members also generally may not receive any compensation from the corporation, such as consulting, advisory, or similar fees, other than their compensation for serving as directors and board committee members.

Typically, audit committees consist of three to five independent directors. The U.S. stock exchanges require that the audit committee have at least three members. The U.S. stock exchanges also require that all committee members be financially literate and that at least one audit committee member have accounting or financial management experience.

In addition, federal securities laws require a public company to disclose whether any member of its audit committee qualifies as an "audit committee financial expert," a term defined in SEC rules and focused on accounting and auditing knowledge and experience. If the committee does not have such an expert, the corporation must disclose that fact and the reason for not having such an expert. If the board determines that a committee member qualifies as an audit committee financial expert, the corporation must disclose the name of the member and state whether that member is independent. Because of these requirements, most public companies have at least one audit committee member who qualifies as an audit committee financial expert. Directors who are designated as audit committee financial experts should be personally satisfied that they meet those requirements.

It is important that all audit committee members have a sufficient understanding of financial reporting and internal control principles to provide informed oversight. New audit committee members are expected to become familiar with key financial issues, critical accounting policies, and accounting practices in the industry or industries in which the corporation operates. Moreover, it is good practice for all committee members to be regularly updated on significant developments in financial reporting and controls through briefings by internal financial officers, the independent auditors, and/or legal counsel.

B. PRINCIPAL FUNCTIONS

Federal securities laws and U.S. stock exchange listing standards establish many of the audit committee's duties and responsibilities, the most significant of which involve engaging an external auditor and overseeing the audit. Audit committees may assume other functions as determined by the board. Public companies must have a formal, written charter for the audit committee specifying its duties and responsibilities. It is good practice for the committee to review its charter annually. The corporation must either publish the charter on its website and disclose the website address or, at least once every three years, include the charter as an exhibit to its proxy statement.

Audit committee members will want to understand the tasks in the charter and develop a schedule for performing those tasks. For information, audit committees generally rely on management, including the corporation's accounting, finance, treasury, internal audit, and legal staff, as well as the corporation's external auditor. At public companies, the committee also has the authority to retain its own accountants, attorneys, or other advisors. The federal securities laws require the corporation to pay for these advisors.

Key duties of public company audit committees include:

- selecting and engaging the corporation's external auditor;
- evaluating the auditor's independence, qualifications, and performance (including those of the engagement partner and other senior members of the audit staff);
- reviewing and approving annually the proposed terms of the external auditor's engagement, including the scope and plan of the audit and the fee arrangements;
- approving, before each engagement, any additional audit-related or non-audit services to be provided by the audit firm, based on the committee's judgment as to whether the firm is an appropriate choice to provide the additional services and whether the engagement might involve prohibited non-audit services or impair the firm's independence;
- providing oversight of the internal audit function (NYSE-listed companies);
- overseeing the corporation's compliance with legal and regulatory requirements (if there is no separate compliance committee);
- establishing procedures to receive and respond to any complaints or concerns about the corporation's accounting, internal controls, or auditing matters, and assuring that there are procedures for the confidential and anonymous submission by employees of such complaints or concerns;
- discussing with management the corporation's quarterly and annual earnings press releases, including consideration of any financial information presented in the release that is not in accordance with generally accepted accounting principles (GAAP);
- reviewing the corporation's quarterly and annual financial statements, management certifications, and related disclosures with both management and the external auditor and discussing with

each of them any significant issues regarding choice of accounting principles, financial statement presentation, or the quality of management's accounting judgments;
- determining whether to recommend to the board that the audited annual financial statements be included in the corporation's annual report on Form 10-K;
- considering, in consultation with the external auditor and any senior internal audit executive, the adequacy and effectiveness of the corporation's internal controls, which, among other things, must be designed to provide reasonable assurance that the corporation's books and records are accurate, its assets are safeguarded, and the publicly reported financial statements prepared by management are presented fairly and in conformity with GAAP;
- reviewing management's annual assessment of the effectiveness of the corporation's internal controls over financial reporting and the external auditor's audit of the effectiveness of those controls;
- meeting quarterly in executive session with the external auditor to discuss any concerns the auditor has with management's accounting or financial reporting judgments and any audit problems or difficulties experienced in the audit and management's response thereto;
- reviewing and approving the audit committee's annual report to shareholders required to be included in a public company's annual meeting proxy statement;
- discussing policies with respect to risk assessment and risk management; and
- reporting regularly to the board of directors on the committee's activities.

C. ENGAGING THE AUDITORS AND PRE-APPROVING THEIR SERVICES

One of the key roles of the audit committee is to engage and oversee the corporation's external auditor. The audit committee reviews and approves the terms of engagement and compensation and needs to understand the scope of the audit. For public companies, the audit committee must pre-approve all audit and non-audit services the external auditor performs during the year, as well as any audit-related services performed by any other auditing firm. The pre-approval process allows the committee and its advisors to consider the effect of any additional audit or non-audit work on the auditor's independence. In addition, for public companies, the external auditor must provide an annual letter about its independence to the audit committee. The committee must discuss this letter with the external auditor and consider the effect, if any, of non-audit work performed by the auditor on the auditor's independence.

Many audit committees develop policies and procedures to pre-approve specific types of audit and non-audit services before the need for an engagement arises. For public companies, the audit committee must pre-approve all tax services and internal control-related services engagement by engagement. Some committees delegate this pre-approval authority to the chair (or a subcommittee) of the audit committee to ensure that necessary services proceed efficiently, allowing for approval between audit committee meetings. Any individual or subcommittee that has this authority must report all decisions to the full committee.

D. OVERSEEING THE INDEPENDENT AUDIT

The audit committee is responsible for evaluating annually the effectiveness of the external auditor, including reviewing the auditor's letter confirming its independence and discussing the firm's independence with the auditor, the auditor's knowledge of the financial issues and accounting standards of the industry or industries in which the corporation operates, and the timeliness and quality of the auditor's services. This evaluation includes discussing with the external auditor the results of the most recent annual evaluation of the audit firm by the Public Company Accounting Oversight Board (PCAOB).

The audit committee has an ongoing role with respect to the annual audit. During the planning phase of the annual audit, the committee meets with the external auditor to review the plan for the staffing, scope, and cost of the audit and to discuss any areas that may require emphasis or special procedures during the audit. As the annual audit is completed, the audit committee reviews the external auditor's draft opinion letter, including with respect to any critical audit matters identified in the opinion. The committee also reviews with the external auditor any problems or difficulties encountered, any significant issues requiring discussion or debate with management during or after the audit, and the letter from the external auditor to management summarizing audit observations.

The audit committee needs to understand significant accounting judgments and estimates that materially affect the corporation's financial statements. Corporations sometimes have a choice among available generally accepted accounting principles. Therefore, the committee will want to inquire about and understand the effect of alternative choices on reported results. The audit committee reviews, annually or as frequently as needed, with the external auditor and with the CFO or chief accounting officer, any significant issues regarding, and any changes in, choices of accounting principles. The committee also needs to review with the auditor the auditor's assessment of the quality of management's accounting judgments and estimates.

The audit committee generally discusses, with the participation of the corporation's CFO and senior internal audit executive, any significant deficiencies or material weaknesses the external auditor identified during its annual audit of internal controls. If the external auditor identifies any significant deficiencies or material weaknesses, the audit committee should oversee management's timely remediation of those deficiencies or weaknesses.

The above-discussed processes and reviews allow the audit committee of a public company to determine whether to recommend to the board inclusion of the audited financial statements in the corporation's annual report in accordance with SEC rules.

E. INTERACTION WITH INTERNAL AUDIT

The NYSE requires its listed companies to have an internal audit function. Many Nasdaq-listed companies also have an in-house internal audit function. Internal auditors typically are employees of the corporation, but some corporations outsource some or all of this function to a firm that is not affiliated with their external auditors. Any internal audit function will usually operate under a written charter approved by the audit committee.

The audit committee routinely meets, in private, with the senior internal audit executive to discuss the relationship between the internal and external audit programs, to consider any problems or issues that may have occurred since the last meeting, and to review the implementation of any corrective actions recommended to management by internal audit. Before the fiscal year begins, the audit committee should approve the annual internal audit plan. The audit committee needs to ensure that the internal audit function has sufficient staff resources and budget to fulfill its internal audit plan for the coming year.

F. MEETINGS WITH AUDITORS

Although the CFO and chief accounting officer normally attend meetings with external and internal auditors, the audit committee will also meet with the external and internal auditors in executive session, without management present. The NYSE requires the audit committees of listed companies to meet periodically with each of the external auditor and the senior internal audit executive. These sessions typically address whether:

- the auditors are uncomfortable with any financial management practices in financial reporting decisions;
- the auditors have had any significant disagreements with management, including with respect to critical audit matters;
- the auditors have had full cooperation of management throughout the audit process;
- the corporation has reasonably effective accounting systems and controls in place; and
- the auditor recommends strengthening any material systems or controls or financial staffing.

Many audit committees find it useful to have the external auditor describe areas that involved the most discussion with management during the course of the auditor's work. Audit committees may also meet separately with management to discuss management's assessment of the quality of services provided by the external and internal auditors.

The audit committee should understand, and discuss with the external auditor and management, their respective roles with respect to the corporation's quarterly financial reports. The audit committee should also establish with the external auditor a process for promptly raising with the committee or its chair significant deficiencies or material weaknesses in internal control over financial reporting and critical audit matters as they arise.

As part of the external auditor's annual audit of the corporation's internal control over financial reporting, the external auditor must assess whether the audit committee understands and exercises its oversight responsibility over financial reporting and internal controls. As part of this assessment, the external auditor will consider the audit committee's knowledge about the corporation's accounting policies and internal controls and ability to monitor any control remediation efforts by management. If the auditor concludes that the audit committee's oversight is ineffective, the auditor must report that conclusion, in writing, to the board.

G. OTHER FUNCTIONS THAT MAY BE PERFORMED BY AUDIT COMMITTEES

Board oversight duties and responsibilities on which the audit committee often takes the lead include:

- establishing and overseeing policies related to, and approving (in coordination with the corporation's nominating and governance committee) related person transactions between the corporation and its officers or directors, or their family members or enterprises any of them control;
- providing input in the hiring, compensation, performance review, and reassignment or termination of the senior internal audit executive;
- approving internal audit plans and reviewing and approving the budget for the internal audit group;
- if the audit committee also oversees compliance, receiving regular compliance reports at each meeting;
- reviewing the external auditor's management letter and management's responses to that letter (which generally includes comments on any control deficiencies observed during the audit and other recommendations arising from the audit);
- receiving reports on significant matters considered by the corporation's disclosure committee, if any;
- meeting in executive sessions with the corporation's legal counsel to review pending claims and litigation, possible loss contingencies, and other legal concerns, including the status of pending litigation and procedures and policies for addressing legal and compliance issues and reduction of legal risk; and
- meeting in executive session each quarter with the CFO, chief accounting officer, chief compliance officer, and senior internal audit executive.

H. MEETINGS WITH COMPLIANCE OFFICERS

Unless there is another board committee responsible for compliance oversight, the audit committee will receive reports from and meet regularly with the officers responsible for implementing the corporation's code of business conduct and compliance policies. Officers with compliance responsibilities may include the general counsel, the senior internal audit executive, and the chief compliance officer. Meetings with such officers should take place in executive sessions outside the presence of other officers and any management directors. The scope and content of those reports and meetings should give the committee timely information about the number and types of concerns reported and investigated, any material violations of law or corporate policies, any disciplinary actions taken, and any other information to enable the committee to monitor the effectiveness of the overall compliance program. These officers generally report to the committee annually (or more frequently, if appropriate) on how the elements of the compliance program satisfy applicable legal requirements.

In addition, the general counsel will want to meet regularly with the audit committee (or other committee responsible for compliance oversight), in executive session, to communicate any concerns or material updates regarding litigation and legal compliance matters, including potential or ongoing material violations of law by the corporation and senior manager breaches of fiduciary duties, violation of corporate policies, and ethical violations.

I. ESTABLISHING PROCEDURES TO HANDLE COMPLAINTS

Under federal law and SEC regulations, the audit committee of a public company must assure that the corporation has procedures for employees to report anonymously and confidentially concerns or complaints about accounting, internal controls, and auditing matters, as well as violations of the corporation's code of ethics. Corporations operating outside the United States may need to ensure that these procedures comply with the privacy regimes of other countries.

The committee works with management to create and oversee procedures adequate to ensure that information reaches the committee in a form conducive to identifying "red flags" and to ensuring timely and efficient review and resolution of any issues. For example, the audit committee may decide to rely on an ethics or compliance officer to gather, review, and process information, or it may decide to outsource this task to a third-party service provider.

Under federal law and SEC regulations, lawyers for public companies (both internal and outside counsel) may be required to report to a committee of independent directors, or to the board, if they have credible reason to believe there has been a material violation of securities laws by the corporation or any of its officers, directors, employees, or agents. The boards of public companies may determine that the audit committee is the appropriate committee to receive such reports. If so, the audit committee will want to have an effective process for acting on such reports, including an understanding about arranging for legal advice from outside counsel when appropriate.

J. MEETINGS, TIME COMMITMENT, AND COMPENSATION

The audit committee discusses and determines the number of meetings it needs to hold to discharge its responsibilities effectively. U.S. stock exchange listing standards require audit committees to review quarterly and annual reports filed with the SEC. It is common and a good practice for public company audit committees to have an in-person or virtual meeting with the corporation's CEO, CFO, and external auditor in advance of each quarterly earnings release. As a result, most audit committees schedule four or more in-person or virtual meetings per year. It is important that the schedules for board and other committee meetings and activities allow sufficient time for audit committee deliberations.

Membership on the audit committee requires a significant time commitment. Many public company boards provide their audit committee members with additional compensation beyond the base compensation for directors serving on other committees to compensate audit committee members for the large time commitment audit committee service involves.

CHAPTER 9 Compensation Committee

The compensation committee is responsible for oversight of the executive compensation process. Executive compensation plays a significant role in attracting, retaining, and motivating the management talent critical to the corporation's success and is subject to scrutiny by the SEC, stock exchanges, courts, and proxy advisory firms. Unlike other areas, where directors rely to a large extent on management to implement the corporation's strategy, management has a conflict when it comes to executive compensation. Therefore, the independence of the decision makers, and the integrity and transparency of the decision-making process, are critically important.

In performing its decision-making and risk management functions, the compensation committee should consider relevant factors, including the following questions:

- How are compensation packages for the CEO and other executive officers determined?
- Is management's compensation reasonably related to appropriate evaluation metrics?
- Does the compensation structure appropriately motivate management to achieve strategic objectives and build value for shareholders while encouraging legal compliance and behaviors in line with desired corporate culture?

- Do a corporation's public disclosures provide accuracy and transparency regarding the nature of, and the reasoning behind, executive compensation decisions?
- Are severance, change-of-control, and post-employment benefits appropriately correlated to corporate interests and reasonable in amount?

A. MEMBERSHIP

The members of the compensation committee should be qualified to act with independence and meet any applicable membership requirements imposed by U.S. stock exchange listing standards. U.S. stock exchange listing standards require that the compensation committee consist solely of independent directors. These independence standards are more stringent than those applicable to directors generally. In addition, for equity compensation programs, SEC rules provide exemptions for equity grants made by a committee composed entirely of "non-employee directors," which are similar to, but not the same as, "independent directors." Consequently, the eligibility of prospective compensation committee members should be reviewed against each applicable standard.

Interlocking compensation committee memberships should also be avoided. For example, if an executive officer of a corporation serves on the compensation committee of another corporation, and an executive officer of that other corporation serves on the first corporation's compensation committee, they are interlocking. Interlocking compensation committee memberships are undesirable because they trigger additional proxy statement disclosures and may disqualify a director from independent status under listing standards.

Even when a director meets the applicable independence requirements, close personal or business ties between the director and the CEO may result in, or at least create the appearance of, conflicts of interest that would indicate the director is not an appropriate member of the compensation committee. However, these relationships standing alone are not necessarily deemed to impede independence.

B. PRINCIPAL FUNCTIONS

Compensation committee members should review the compensation committee charter to familiarize themselves with the duties of the compensation committee. Typically, compensation committees:

- oversee the corporation's overall executive compensation programs and assess whether they establish appropriate incentives for executive officers;
- review and approve goals and objectives established for CEO and executive officer compensation that align with board-approved corporate goals and objectives and annually evaluate executive performance in light of those goals and objectives;
- approve the compensation and benefits of the CEO and certain other executive officers;
- assess how compensation policies and programs contribute to or affect the corporation's risk profile and structure them to create incentives for management to make risk-appropriate decisions;
- evaluate and approve compensatory arrangements applicable to executive officers, such as employment agreements and change-of-control agreements;
- establish and periodically review policies for the administration of executive compensation programs (including all equity-based plans and perquisites);
- administer incentive compensation plans and equity-based plans generally;
- consider the results of advisory say-on-pay votes and advisory say-on-pay-frequency votes (which are discussed below); and
- review any required disclosures regarding executive compensation programs.

C. OPERATION OF THE COMPENSATION COMMITTEE

1. Decision-Making Process

The compensation committee typically receives input from management and external advisors with respect to compensation programs. The committee then independently deliberates and determines whether to approve the proposed compensation program. For example, while a CEO will review his or her performance and the performance of the senior executive team, a member of management should never be present during deliberations regarding his or her own compensation. The committee should consider the CEO's compensation in a private session, without the CEO or the CEO's subordinate officers present. Independent compensation consultants or counsel typically are present throughout compensation committee meetings, including during these executive sessions, in the compensation committee's discretion.

2. Independent Advice

U.S. stock exchange listing standards require that committees have the power to hire (without management influence in the selection process) compensation consultants, legal advisors, and other experts. These outside advisors provide market data and advice that is independent of corporate personnel or management-selected outside specialists for advice and guidance.

Given the significance of executive compensation and corporate governance at public companies, SEC rules require compensation committees to consider specific independence factors before retaining or receiving the advice of outside advisors, including the following:

- other services performed by the advisor for the corporation;
- fees paid to the advisor, as a percentage of the advisor's total revenue;
- the advisor's policies and procedures that are designed to prevent conflicts of interest; and
- existing personal and business relationships between the advisor and the corporation's executive officers or members of the compensation committee.

Regardless of whether the committee engages outside compensation consultants or counsel for assistance, the committee is ultimately responsible for approving the terms, amounts, and forms of compensation and cannot substitute the advice of advisors for its own business judgment.

3. Structure and Components of Executive Compensation

A significant portion of an executive's compensation should be tied to the achievement of the corporation's strategic objectives and financial performance. Setting long-term and short-term goals creates a balanced perspective and can reward appropriate progress as well as attainment. Benchmarking against peer companies is sometimes used as a tool when setting or reviewing executive compensation, but the committee should avoid simply matching the design or amounts of compensation at peer companies and be mindful of differentiating factors such as the corporation's culture, values, and desired behaviors.

Compensation packages typically consist of cash, equity (or equity-derived instruments), and benefits. Equity can consist of restricted stock, restricted stock units, stock appreciation rights, and stock options. In choosing the attributes and conditions of an award, compensation committees should:

- consider whether the award provides the intended incentive and is appropriately linked to performance of the executive and the corporation;
- understand the financial, accounting, and tax impacts on the corporation; and
- understand the calculation and achievement of any financial performance metrics and targets.

A good practice is to obtain audit committee review of the calculations for financial performance metrics before the compensation committee reviews and approves any annual cash or equity incentive compensation awards. For these reasons, boards may choose to have some overlapping membership between the audit and compensation committees.

The compensation committee should also review the benefits and perquisites (often called perks) provided to executive officers, particularly when approving employment contracts. Perks have received considerable attention due to perceived excesses in their use, such as personal use of corporate aircraft, tax gross-ups, and use of corporation resources post-employment. The SEC's rules require public companies to disclose perks provided to a named executive officer (unless the value of all perks provided to the officer is less than $10,000 in value, in the aggregate). Other important areas of scrutiny are front-loaded equity grants, retirement benefits, termination payments, and change-in-control benefits. There is widespread shareholder concern that this compensation is not sufficiently related to job performance or value creation for the corporation, and compensation committees should be aware of the relationship between these benefits and corporate financial performance.

The compensation committee also has a role in risk oversight for public company compensation policies and practices. Under SEC rules, public companies must analyze their compensation policies and practices and disclose whether those policies and practices encourage excessive risk taking or are reasonably likely to have a material adverse effect on the corporation. In most corporations, management, in some cases working with compensation consultants, prepares this analysis and makes the initial determination regarding the companies' policies and practices by tallying all elements of compensation, determining the risks posed by each element, and then analyzing any mitigating factors. The compensation committee, however, retains an oversight role, and management should detail its procedures and provide the committee with a summary of management's analysis and determination. The compensation committee may want to review and approve management's analysis or even conduct its own analysis with input from its compensation consultants.

4. Documentation of Approval of Executive Compensation

The compensation committee should review with senior management the corporation's procedures for accurately and timely documenting the grants or issuances of equity awards, both in the compensation committee's minutes (or other written action) and in the documentation evidencing the awards. Compensation committee minutes or resolutions that adequately discuss the compensation committee's rationale, deliberation, and consideration regarding the grants or issuances of equity awards and any other form of executive compensation are considered good practice and can assist the corporation in preparing, if required, SEC disclosures regarding the process. As a general matter, a corporation should also have adequate written procedures relating to the grant or issuance of equity awards, including timing and pricing, to help protect the corporation, its executives, and the compensation committee against claims of manipulation or abuse. Good practices also include granting equity awards pursuant to a program, plan, or practice, such as at pre-scheduled meetings or on a predetermined date. These practices can mitigate against potential timing issues related to the release of material non-public information or blackout periods for employee trading of corporation securities.

5. Regulations Regarding Executive Compensation

The compensation committee should become familiar with and receive legal advice about legal restrictions on officer and director compensation. Federal securities law prohibits most personal loans and extensions or arrangements of credit from a public company to its directors and executive officers. In addition, the U.S. stock exchanges require listed companies to have policies providing for the recoupment of incentive-based compensation received by executive officers preceding an accounting restatement that results from material non-compliance with financial reporting requirements, even where the executive officers have not engaged in any misconduct. The SEC may also seek recoupment of other compensation and profits from the sale of securities from executive officers following accounting restatements.

The compensation committee should determine, and incorporate into a formal policy, the circumstances under which the corporation would be entitled to recoup compensation. The policy should specify the covered employees and types and amounts of compensation subject to the policy, as well as address how the policy will be implemented, taking into consideration the corporation's ability to enforce the policy under relevant law.

Compensation committees should consider whether they are or should be fiduciaries with respect to the corporation's pension, 401(k), or other employee benefit plans that are subject to regulation under the Employee Retirement Income Security Act (ERISA). Under ERISA, plan fiduciaries are subject to heightened scrutiny and responsibility with respect to the investment of plan assets. The compensation committee has a duty to be informed about the corporation's compensation and benefit structure, but most compensation committees do not act as fiduciaries for ERISA-covered benefit plans.

D. DISCLOSURE OF COMPENSATION DECISIONS

The annual meeting proxy statement or annual report on Form 10-K for most public companies includes detailed information, in tabular form, about the compensation paid to executives. It must also include a Compensation Discussion and Analysis (CD&A) section, which is a detailed discussion of the key elements of the corporation's executive compensation.

The topics the CD&A addresses include:

- the objectives of the corporation's compensation program;
- what the compensation program is designed to reward;
- each element of compensation;
- how the corporation determines the amount (and the formula, if any) for each element of pay; and
- how each compensation element fits into the corporation's overall compensation.

Independent compensation consultants and others typically assist in the preparation of the CD&A. Because the committee makes decisions for senior executives outside the presence of management, the committee should assist management in its preparation of the CD&A and should review the disclosure to confirm it reflects and highlights the various factors the compensation committee weighed and considered. The compensation committee must state, in a separate report in the proxy statement, that its members have reviewed and discussed the CD&A with management and based on this review and discussion, recommended that it be included in the proxy statement.

SEC rules require most public companies to make specific compensation disclosures in addition to the CD&A. Some of the more notable disclosures include:

- the compensation committee's retention of any consultants;
- the relationship between executive compensation actually paid and financial performance; and
- the total annual compensation of the CEO and the median total annual compensation of all employees, and the ratio of the two.

The compensation committee obtains advice from management and legal counsel about compliance with law and applicable exchange listing standards.

Public companies are required to have several non-binding shareholder votes that relate to executive compensation. First, public companies must hold a non-binding shareholder vote (a so-called "say-on-pay vote") to approve compensation of the "named executive officers" (as defined in SEC rules) for intervals specified in a shareholder vote but at least once every three years. Second, public companies must also hold a non-binding shareholder vote every six years to determine whether say-on-pay votes will be every one, two, or three years. Because of the popularity of "say-on-pay votes" with institutional shareholders and proxy advisory firms, nearly every public company has an annual say-on-pay vote. Finally, public companies must hold a non-binding shareholder vote to approve so-called "golden parachute" compensation in connection with a solicitation for a shareholder meeting to approve an acquisition, merger, consolidation, or sale of substantially all of their assets.

E. DIRECTOR COMPENSATION

Decisions about director compensation generally reside with the entire board. Usually, it is more efficient for the board to delegate director compensation to either the compensation committee or the nominating and governance committee, either of which would ultimately make a recommendation on a director compensation program to the board for its review and approval. The committee making the recommendations typically seeks the advice of an independent compensation consultant.

The director compensation program should fairly compensate directors for their service, while guarding against the potential for claims or challenges that such compensation is excessive or impairs non-management director independence. Directors have an unavoidable conflict of interest in fixing their own compensation, and they cannot eliminate the conflict by having management or an independent compensation consultant suggest the director compensation programs. Directors nevertheless have the responsibility to determine their own compensation, so they must ensure they engage in a thorough, deliberative decision-making process and can demonstrate they have considered the information or received independent advice necessary to reach a fair decision. In setting their own compensation, directors should be mindful that doing so is an interested transaction subject to heightened judicial review if challenged, and, therefore, they may consider taking extra care to justify the decision made. In some circumstances, seeking shareholder approval or ratification of director compensation may be appropriate to protect the action.

Director compensation may take several different forms, including annual stock or cash retainers, attendance fees for board and committee meetings, deferred compensation plans, restricted stock, restricted stock units, and stock options. Additional compensation for additional service, such as for serving as independent board chair, lead independent director, chair of a committee, member of a special committee, or member of a particularly active committee, is also customary. The corporation's executives who serve as directors generally do not receive additional compensation for board service.

To align director compensation with shareholder value, many public companies grant awards of restricted stock or restricted stock units. Many corporations have stock ownership guidelines requiring directors to hold a minimum amount of corporation stock while serving as a director. Directors generally are given a period following initial appointment to meet the stock ownership requirement. In addition, some public companies have included annual limits on director compensation as part of their shareholder-approved equity incentive plan.

Directors should be mindful that they may be either prohibited from selling shares, or strongly discouraged from doing so, until after they have ceased to serve on the board. Even if directors have satisfied stock ownership requirements, they may be discouraged from selling any shares in the corporation because of the signal that insider sales may send to the market. Moreover, directors may be subject to extended prohibitions on trading as a result of their possession of material non-public information.

SEC proxy disclosure rules require detailed disclosure of all elements of director compensation, including any perks (unless the value of all perks provided to the director is less than $10,000 in value, in the aggregate) and charitable donation programs. Any consulting or other agreements with directors and any payments to directors for consulting or other services beyond the regular directors' compensation program can impair independence and require disclosure in the annual proxy statement. The board should be sensitive to and avoid compensation policies or corporate perks that might impair the independence of its non-management directors.

CHAPTER

10 Nominating and Governance Committee

An effective nominating and governance committee is critical to board performance. This committee's stature and importance are tied to the fact that a corporation's investors are often focused on the quality and strength of a corporation's board and governance systems. The committee is responsible for recruiting and maintaining board members with the appropriate skills and independence for quality decision making. The committee also develops and recommends to the board corporate governance principles applicable to the corporation.

A. MEMBERSHIP

Generally, public company nominating and governance committees should be composed solely of independent directors. The NYSE requires each of its listed companies to have a nominating and governance committee composed entirely of independent directors, with a written charter that addresses the committee's purposes and responsibilities. Nasdaq does not require listed companies to have a nominating and governance committee but does require that listed companies have a formal charter or written resolutions addressing the nomination process. Nasdaq also requires that either a committee of independent directors (subject to limited exceptions) or a majority of independent board members select or recommend director nominees. As a practical matter, Nasdaq-listed companies satisfy this requirement with a committee of independent directors.

B. PRINCIPAL FUNCTIONS

The nominating and governance committee typically is responsible for:

- identifying, evaluating, and recommending individuals qualified to become members of the board, consistent with criteria approved by the board;
- selecting or recommending that the board select the director nominees to stand for election at each annual meeting of shareholders of the corporation or to fill vacancies on the board;
- adopting, maintaining, and regularly updating corporate governance principles and policies;
- overseeing the annual performance evaluation of the board and its committees and management; and
- recommending directors to serve on all committees of the board.

Additional key duties of public company nominating and governance committees include:

- developing, recommending to the board, and monitoring a statement of corporate governance principles or guidelines (required of NYSE-listed companies);
- developing proposals for amendments to bylaws, articles or certificate of incorporation, board committee charters, and other governance documents or board-level policies;
- providing oversight of an annual self-evaluation process to determine whether the board, its committees, and, possibly, individual directors are functioning effectively and reporting the results of the self-evaluation process to the board (required of NYSE-listed companies);
- evaluating director standards of independence and monitoring director compliance with those standards;
- providing for director orientation and education programs;
- reviewing, managing, and making recommendations regarding the board's leadership structure;
- reviewing the board committee structure, including each committee's recommendation regarding its charter and size, as well as the possible addition of other committees, such as finance, public policy, investment, risk management, or health, safety, and environmental committees;
- reviewing and making recommendations with respect to the corporation's director policies, such as director compensation (if not addressed by the compensation committee; see Chapter 9 for a

discussion of director compensation), retirement, indemnification, and insurance; and
- establishing and disclosing the corporation's policy and procedures for shareholder communications with directors.

C. CRITERIA FOR BOARD MEMBERSHIP

The nominating and governance committee recommends to the board criteria for identifying appropriate director candidates. These criteria are usually set forth in corporate governance principles or a separate policy. The attributes of an effective corporate director include integrity, strength of character, commitment, candor, common sense, inquisitiveness, leadership, personal accomplishments, objectivity, competence, and independent business judgment. In addition to these personal qualities, there may be desirable individual qualifications, such as technical skills, career specialization, specific industry experience, or expertise in matters such as finance, compensation, or governance. Other important areas of expertise may change over time and may depend on a corporation's specific needs. They may include, for example, expertise in regulatory matters, risk management, and global management. An effective nominating and governance committee seeks director attributes to complement and expand the attributes of the existing board members as well as satisfy legal requirements. There is also an emphasis on diversity considerations, recognizing that diversity can contribute significant value by providing additional perspectives to board deliberations. The articles or certificate of incorporation, bylaws, or board policies may include other qualifications for directors, such as age, length of service limitations, citizenship requirements, or relevant experience.

There is no one-size-fits-all approach to director searches. The desired outcome is a board with diverse experience relevant to the corporation's business that can build consensus and effectively exercise collaborative judgment and, when appropriate, challenge management. Performing rigorous evaluations of the board and individual directors can inform the attributes sought in director searches. Some boards look for specific skills and experiences to build on what they currently possess, lack, or need to strengthen. Developing a skills matrix can be helpful in focusing the search on candidates who can provide needed additional talent and experience to the corporation.

Many corporate governance commentators recommend that a public company board have a substantial majority of independent directors, and the U.S. stock exchanges require at least a majority of directors to be independent (as defined by the applicable exchange). When considering director independence, the committee should review proxy advisory firm positions regarding independence and also bear in mind broader judicial standards of disinterestedness applicable for judicial review of conflicts of interest or other issues. As a result, the committee should evaluate the full range of business and personal relationships between director candidates and the corporation and its senior managers in assessing a candidate's independence.

The nominating and governance committee can help ensure that the board receives candid input from senior management. In addition to input from the CEO, who is typically on the board, the committee should consider how best to access senior management to ensure this input. Some nominating and governance committees determine that certain senior officers, in addition to the CEO, should serve as directors, but this is less common (and increasingly rare for public companies). Others decide that attendance at board or committee meetings by senior officers in a non-director capacity is sufficient to facilitate the board's ready access to information regarding the business and operations of the corporation.

D. EVALUATING BOARD INCUMBENTS

The nominating and governance committee is usually responsible for developing and overseeing the processes for evaluating the board, its committees, and incumbent directors. Tools to assist in the evaluation process may include board, committee, or individual self-evaluations; peer evaluations; and confidential discussions led by the chair, lead independent director, or nominating and governance committee chair. Outside consultants or counsel can also be effective in administering the evaluation process. The committee should assess the contributions and performance of individual directors based on their attendance, preparation, participation, and other relevant factors. The feedback and results gathered from these and other governance processes serve to support the committee's deliberation and consideration of each director's contribution and board needs before deciding whether to recommend renomination of an incumbent director. This practice can help address the common criticism that election or appointment to the board is tantamount to tenure. It is also responsive to SEC rules requiring disclosure of director qualifications relevant to serving on the corporation's board. Conducting board and committee evaluations annually helps to ensure effective performance and oversight.

Boards handle the sensitive issue of board succession and refreshment in a variety of ways. Some boards attempt to address the issue indirectly through the adoption of mandatory retirement policies or limits on tenure, but these policies can create an expectation that board service continues until retirement or the term limit. Long-tenured directors and directors whose relevant experience is not apparent to investors are easy for shareholder activists to attack.

E. NOMINATING DIRECTORS

The nominating and governance committee leads the director recruitment and selection process. The committee approves and selects, or recommends that the board select, director nominees, including both incumbent directors and new candidates. The committee also recommends candidates to the board to fill director vacancies and the addition of new directors between annual meetings.

The committee should seek out candidates and can engage search consultants to assist in identifying appropriate candidates. The committee's charter should give the committee the authority to retain a search firm to identify director candidates, including the authority to approve the search firm's fees and other retention terms. The committee can also look to incumbent directors, including management directors, to suggest candidates for the board. Shareholder engagement may yield suggestions for director candidates (or particular skills, experience, or other characteristics desirable in the boardroom) from the corporation's institutional investors and other shareholders. Where shareholders have recommended candidates or nominated candidates, the committee should vet those candidates in the same way as other candidates. The committee should control the process, including making decisions with respect to nominees and recommending to the board a slate of nominees. Moreover, the committee should be the conduit for communications regarding shareholder recommendations for director candidates. Both the independent board chair, if there is one, or the lead independent director and the nominating and governance committee chair should be prominently involved in the recruiting process to ensure that the committee is making the nominating decisions and not the CEO or other insiders.

Public companies have disclosure obligations with respect to the nomination process and board composition. Public company proxy statements must disclose the nominating and governance committee's procedures and policies for considering director candidates, including the committee's process for identifying and evaluating director candidates, as well as the particular experience, attributes, skills, and qualifications the committee focused on in selecting or recommending each director candidate. Nasdaq-listed companies are required to annually disclose board diversity in a prescribed matrix and disclose whether they have, or explain why they do not have, at least the specified number of diverse directors.

In addition to a summary of this information, some public companies disclose a board skills matrix that indicates how each member contributes specific qualifications, attributes, skills, and experience to the board. Also, public companies must disclose individual profiles of each director, including biographical data, a summary of the individual's professional experience, and an explanation of his or her relevant qualifications, attributes, skills, and experience. The proxy statement requires the board to explain why it believes the nomination of each director nominee is warranted.

Furthermore, public companies must disclose whether, and if so how, the nominating and governance committee considers diversity in identifying director nominees. If the nominating and governance committee has a diversity policy, the corporation must disclose how the policy is applied and how the committee assesses the policy's effectiveness. The purpose of these disclosure requirements is to increase shareholder understanding of the nominating process. Accordingly, the committee should ensure its procedures and policies are consistent with the committee's circumstances and operations and that they are sufficiently formalized to provide clarity and satisfy the scrutiny that follows from public disclosure.

F. RECOMMENDING COMMITTEE MEMBERS AND CHAIRS

The nominating and governance committee also makes recommendations to the board about the responsibilities and composition of all board committees, including committee chairs and the qualifications for membership on committees. Some boards have a policy of periodic rotation of committee memberships among the directors to develop expertise and allocate equitably the time commitment. The nominating and governance committee usually oversees this process.

G. CHIEF EXECUTIVE OFFICER AND OTHER MANAGEMENT SUCCESSION

As discussed in Chapter 7, executive officer succession planning is one of the most important functions of the board. The nominating and governance committee often plays a key role with respect to this function. In performing this role, the committee may review and approve proposed changes in senior management positions, with the understanding that the CEO should have considerable discretion in selecting, retaining, and reviewing members of the management team. To perform these functions, the nominating and governance committee (or another board committee) should, at least annually, review the performance of the CEO and members of senior management.

H. BOARD AND COMMITTEE LEADERSHIP

The nominating and governance committee typically recommends to the board the appropriate leadership structure for the board and who should chair board committees. As discussed in Chapter 7, many companies that do not have an independent board chair often designate an independent director as a lead director. The nominating and governance committee should consider the appropriateness of such a designation and propose a candidate, along with a description of responsibilities, for the board's consideration if the committee determines a lead independent director is appropriate. In many cases, the chair of the nominating and governance committee may be the appropriate person for this leadership role.

Part IV:
Shareholder Matters, Director Liabilities, and Director Protections

CHAPTER 11 The Relationship between the Board and Shareholders

State law generally vests the responsibility for managing the business and affairs of the corporation in the board of directors. Shareholders do not have direct management rights or responsibilities under state law. Instead, shareholders influence the corporation principally by voting in director elections and on certain other fundamental matters. Shareholders of public companies also have the right under U.S. securities laws and, in the case of listed companies, stock exchange listing standards, to vote on various matters, including advisory votes on executive compensation and, under certain circumstances, to request votes on other corporate governance and policy matters. Some institutional shareholders seek to exercise influence through direct communication with management and directors.

The stock of many public companies is owned principally by institutional investors. Many retail investors have only indirect interests in public companies through their investments in mutual funds or exchange-traded funds. Those funds are the shareholders of the companies in which they are invested, and the managers of the funds vote the shares of those companies. Investors in these funds have no direct rights as shareholders of the companies in which the funds have invested.

A. DIRECTOR ELECTIONS

The main way shareholders influence a corporation is through director elections. The degree of influence shareholders can exert through director elections depends on the term for which directors are elected and the voting standard applicable to those elections. In addition, shareholder influence correlates in part with whether director elections are contested.

1. Term

Directors ordinarily serve for a one-year term that expires at the corporation's next annual meeting of shareholders, with all director nominees standing for election each year. Some companies, however, have "staggered," also known as "classified," boards, with directors divided into classes with staggered terms so that not all directors are elected annually. Typically, staggered boards have three classes, with directors having three-year terms, and one-third of the directors standing for election at each annual shareholder meeting. A principal benefit of a staggered board is that it provides greater continuity to the board than when all directors are elected annually. On the other hand, a staggered board may inhibit takeovers and diminish the board's accountability to shareholders. For this reason, at least for large public companies, staggered boards are not common.

2. Voting Standards

Under the laws of most states, directors are elected by plurality vote unless a different standard is specified in the articles or certificate of incorporation or bylaws. Plurality voting means that the candidates with the highest number of votes in their favor (even if less than a majority of those voting) are elected, up to the maximum number of directorships up for election. A plurality voting standard ensures that a director election is "successful" in the sense that all open directorships are filled, and thus avoids a "failed" election when all open directorships are not filled.

Although plurality voting is the predominant standard used for contested elections, many large public companies have adopted a majority voting standard for uncontested director elections. There are different formulations for majority voting, but, in general, it means that in order to be elected, the number of votes cast in favor of a director candidate's election must exceed the number of votes cast against or withheld from the candidate's election. The rationale behind a majority voting standard is that if a candidate in an uncontested election cannot garner a majority of "favorable" votes, the candidate should not be elected.

As a result, many institutional investors and other shareholders favor majority voting in director elections because they see it as enhancing the board's accountability to shareholders. In addition, as discussed below, a majority voting standard in director elections can make even an uncontested election have consequences (e.g., a withhold campaign results in a resignation).

If a corporation adopts a majority voting standard for uncontested director elections, a non-incumbent director candidate who receives more "against" or "withhold" than "for" votes is not elected. By contrast, because under the law of most states a director serves until a successor is elected, an incumbent director who fails to achieve a majority favorable vote in an uncontested election will continue on the board as a "holdover" director. In order to prevent incumbent directors who do not receive the requisite majority vote for reelection from remaining on the board as "holdover" directors, many companies that have a majority voting standard to elect directors also require incumbent directors who do not receive a majority favorable vote in an uncontested election to resign or to offer to resign. These director resignation policies often provide that a resignation for failure to receive a majority favorable vote does not become effective unless accepted by a majority of the members of the board other than the director whose resignation is being considered. Many of these policies also provide a time period and other guidelines for the board to decide whether to accept the resignation.

Some companies retain plurality voting for both contested and uncontested elections but have adopted a director resignation policy for an incumbent director who does not receive a majority favorable vote in an uncontested election. The combination of plurality voting and a director resignation policy is commonly referred to as a "plurality plus" voting standard.

3. Contested Elections

The vast majority of elections for corporate directors are not contested. In a typical election, the board nominates a slate of directors and recommends that the corporation's shareholders vote for the members of that slate. Usually, there is little doubt that all directors will be elected. There are, however, a number of ways in which a director election can be contested—or at least take on some of the characteristics of a contested election.

The traditional way to wage a contested election is through a proxy contest. Although shareholders have the right under state law to nominate their own candidates, for public companies, it is typically necessary to solicit proxies from other shareholders for such candidates to have any chance of being elected. This solicitation must comply with the SEC's proxy solicitation rules, including the filing and distribution of separate proxy materials. The process can be expensive and time-consuming, and the outcome of a proxy contest is often uncertain, particularly in light of the SEC's rules requiring the use of "universal proxy cards" (i.e., proxy cards that list both the board's and the dissident's nominees such that shareholders may pick and choose from all when voting in director elections) if the dissident satisfies certain requirements. Therefore, proxy contests, even those involving so-called "short slates" (i.e., involving fewer dissident nominees than open positions), are not lightly undertaken.

Many companies—particularly large publicly traded companies—have adopted proxy access bylaw provisions that provide another opportunity for contested elections. Typically, under proxy access bylaws, shareholders who meet certain requirements (e.g., holding three percent of the corporation's outstanding shares for at least three years) have the right to include a limited number of nominees in the corporation's proxy statement. Proxy access provides an opportunity for a contested election without the shareholders needing to file and disseminate separate proxy materials.

Finally, public company shareholders may conduct "withhold the vote" (or "vote against") campaigns in which they urge other shareholders to vote against some or all of the slate of directors nominated by the board. This is a way for shareholders to express disapproval of board candidates, board oversight, or board policies without nominating other candidates. These campaigns can be relatively easy and inexpensive for a shareholder to conduct—a formal proxy solicitation is not required, and in some cases all the shareholder does is issue a press release. If successful, these campaigns can have direct consequences at a company with a majority voting standard or with a director resignation policy in denying one or more directors a majority favorable vote. And, in any event, even if all directors are reelected, the issues raised in withhold campaigns can be catalysts for change in board composition, structure, and corporate policies.

B. SHAREHOLDER RELATIONS

Public companies communicate with their shareholders in a variety of ways, which include:

- SEC required public reports, which contain information about the company's business operations, financial condition and performance, material developments in those areas on an ongoing basis, and, when shareholders are being solicited for votes, information regarding those matters;

- investor meetings and industry or sector conferences at which companies provide business information;
- press releases;
- ESG reports; and
- other public releases of business information through various media, such as videos, podcasts, social media, and websites.

Communications with shareholders of public companies are subject to legal restrictions. In particular, directors must be mindful of the federal and state securities law anti-fraud provisions and SEC Regulation FD, which prohibits selective disclosure of material non-public information to shareholders or potential investors in non-public settings. Because of Regulation FD, public companies typically will provide public access to investor conferences at which executives are speaking, and file written investor presentations with the SEC, so they are available to all shareholders at the same time.

1. Shareholder Engagement by Management

The primary areas of shareholder engagement involve discussions relating to the corporation's financial performance, business operations, and strategy. Management, including the CEO, CFO, or investor relations department, generally handles this engagement through meetings (in person or through electronic media) with investors.

Another area of shareholder engagement involves matters to be voted on at annual shareholder meetings, such as director elections, executive compensation, and shareholder proposals. In addition, environmental, social, and governance matters (e.g., board diversity, composition, and refreshment) are frequently the subject of shareholder engagement. This engagement is typically handled by management, including the corporate secretary or investor relations personnel, as well as other subject matter experts. It is also common, however, for the board or a board committee to be involved in or oversee that engagement.

Who handles investor relations usually depends on the size of the corporation. Large public companies often have separate investor relations officers or departments. Smaller companies may include investor relations functions within the responsibilities of other officers, such as the CEO or CFO, or an outside investor relations firm.

In general, the purpose of the investor relations function is to provide accurate and consistent information and messaging about the corporation's operations and financial performance to the investment community. Just as important, the goal of investor relations is for the corporation's share price to reflect the corporation's fundamental value. Investor relations personnel should know the corporation's significant investors and equity research analysts and understand their goals and priorities. The investor relations function often determines if investors and analysts would be amenable to specific outreach, coordinates that outreach, and establishes a procedure by which communications received from investors and analysts are reviewed and reported to management and the board or a committee of the board.

Investor relations personnel also may be involved in reviewing the corporation's public filings and other communications with shareholders. This typically includes the investor relations section of the corporation's website. Both the corporation's website and its proxy statement often disclose the corporation's shareholder engagement policies and goals, the people involved in the corporation's shareholder outreach efforts, and a contact for shareholders to ask questions or raise concerns.

The amount and timing of shareholder engagement and those involved vary from corporation to corporation. Some companies wait for investors to approach them; others find benefit in proactively seeking meetings with certain shareholders. Although larger corporations may be able to engage with large institutional investors during the annual meeting season, companies seeking such engagement may find that the governance professionals of institutional shareholders are more available in the off-season than during annual meeting season. As a result, shareholder engagement is often a year-round function.

2. Shareholder Engagement by Directors

Shareholders may wish to engage directly with one or more members of the board on any of a number of subjects. For example, institutional shareholders may be concerned about the corporation's operating strategy, management's performance, or strategic alternatives. They may also wish to discuss topics that are the responsibility of the independent members of the board, such as CEO succession planning, executive compensation, board composition, or other governance matters. Further, as part of their focus on board competence and composition, shareholders may want to gain first-hand knowledge of the individuals serving on a corporation's board. Some institutional investors expect that a corporation will provide access to at least some of its independent directors. Most also expect directors to attend annual shareholder meetings and to be available to answer questions at those meetings.

Companies may have corporate governance guidelines or other policies that address communication by individual board members with shareholders and other third parties. The policies and protocols for director-shareholder engagement best suited to a corporation will depend on many factors, including the nature and extent of existing relationships with investors (including the level of share ownership of the requesting investor), as well as the preferences of investors and directors. Directors should understand the policies and procedures the corporation has in place for communications with shareholders, consult with the corporation's legal department and investor relations personnel about any questions, and make sure any communications are consistent with such policies and procedures and comply with Regulation FD.

Meetings or discussions between directors and shareholders are often preceded by preparatory communications among management, outside counsel and advisors, and relevant board members. Following any meeting with shareholders, the officers or directors involved will normally report back on the topics discussed, any questions or concerns raised or actions requested, and next steps. Depending on the importance of the subjects covered in the meeting(s), management may prepare a summary and distribute it to the board or an appropriate board committee.

3. Proxy Voting Advisory Firms

Institutional investors that do not have in-house voting policy resources may either rely on the recommendations of proxy voting advisory firms regarding how to vote on matters at shareholder meetings or work with proxy voting advisory firms to develop customized voting policies. Even institutional investors that do maintain in-house proxy voting teams may subscribe to and consider the voting recommendations of proxy voting advisory firms.

Proxy voting advisory firms have policies on a variety of corporate governance items and publish ratings that score a corporation's corporate governance against these policies. Governance items covered include board diversity, executive compensation practices, shareholder rights, audit and risk oversight, and ESG matters. Proxy advisory firms update policies annually based on trends and developments. They may recommend voting against, or withholding a vote for, the full board or voting against, or withholding a vote for, a director if a corporation's governance is inconsistent with their policies on a particular matter and that director is a member of a board committee responsible for that matter.

Proxy voting advisory firms also provide influential voting recommendations on shareholder proposals. Even if a shareholder proposal does not pass, the proxy voting advisory firms will often recommend a vote against some or all of the incumbent directors in future elections if the proposal receives significant support but is not implemented or otherwise addressed by the corporation.

Those responsible for engaging with institutional shareholders should understand which of the corporation's institutional investors rely on which of the proxy voting advisory firms in determining how to vote. They should also know the criteria applied by the applicable proxy voting advisory firms in deciding how to vote. In addition, companies may want to communicate directly with proxy voting advisory firms to make sure the information the firms are using about the corporation is accurate.

4. Activist Investors

One category of investors that receives considerable public attention is the activist investor. These investors look for companies trading at a discount to their fundamental values where there may be opportunities to increase stock prices through various corporate actions, such as share repurchases, spinoffs, capital reallocation, business strategy revisions, or sale transactions. Not all activist investors are alike—some have long-term investment horizons and devote a large amount of resources to analyzing their targeted companies, but others have short-term investment horizons and are looking for near-immediate unlocking of value that they believe is not reflected in the corporation's share price. Tactics vary as well, with some activist investors being more aggressive than others.

Activist investors often request or threaten a change to board composition. A request for board representation may be combined with a threat to initiate a proxy contest to replace some or all incumbent board members with directors more open to the investor's proposals. In recent years, most of the candidates proposed by activists have been "independent" of the activist in the sense that they are usually not employees of the activist firm. When an activist succeeds in obtaining board representation, it has most often been through a settlement with the corporation rather than through a proxy contest carried to a final vote, although a number of such proxy contests happen every year.

To be prepared for activist investors, boards of public companies may assemble teams of internal and external advisors, including outside counsel and investment banking, proxy solicitation, and investor relations and communication firms. These teams can provide boards with periodic briefings on activist investor trends and the corporation's vulnerabilities to and preparedness for activist involvement. As a matter of good governance, many boards proactively consider the corporation from the perspective of an activist investor and either preemptively address potential activist campaign platforms or purposefully determine not to do so.

CHAPTER

12 Director Liabilities and Protections

Directors may incur personal liability for breaches of their duty of care or their duty of loyalty or for failure to satisfy other legal or regulatory requirements, including the federal securities laws. Corporations may provide for limitations on these potential liabilities, and may also provide directors (and officers) with indemnification rights and insurance against liabilities and litigation expenses. These provisions allow directors to focus on performing their duties without undue concern over potential personal liability. Directors should periodically review the corporation's indemnification and insurance protections as applicable to both directors and officers.

A. SOURCES OF LIABILITY

1. Corporate Law Liability

Directors have two primary functions: decision making and oversight. Corporate law generally provides that, in performing these functions, directors are fiduciaries and, therefore, have both a duty of care and a duty of loyalty. Directors may in theory be liable for violating either of these duties, but nearly all public (and many private) corporations formed in U.S. jurisdictions have, through their articles or certificate of incorporation, precluded monetary liability for directors who breach the duty of care. Prospective directors should inquire about the extent to which the corporation has eliminated such liability under applicable state law.

Directors in most jurisdictions may, however, be subject to monetary liability for breaching the duty of loyalty. For example, directors may incur liability when they have a conflicting personal interest or are dominated or controlled by a person or entity with such a conflict. Directors should be alert to such conflicts, particularly in corporations with controlling shareholders and in change-in-control transactions—where courts are especially sensitive to compliance with the duty of loyalty. There are several measures available to directors to address these concerns, including disclosure of potential conflicts, recusal, reference to independent committees and advisors, and fully informed shareholder votes. In addition to liability involving a conflict of interest, directors may incur liability for breach of the duty of loyalty when their inattention to their duties rises to a level constituting bad faith or conscious disregard for their duties. Thus, it is important for directors to be actively engaged in discussions and deliberations after having gathered relevant information for board action. Good recordkeeping of board procedure and deliberations is important in protecting directors from liability, especially when, in retrospect, business decisions with poor outcomes can appear to have resulted from conflicts or inattention.

In addition to liability for breach of duties, directors may also be personally liable for authorizing stock repurchases, dividends, or other distributions. This area requires particular caution, as directors may be liable for even simple negligence—a lower standard than typically applicable to liability for breaching fiduciary duties. Whenever there is any question as to a corporation's solvency, directors should obtain appropriate financial and legal advice before approving stock repurchases, dividends, or other distributions to shareholders. This advice may include requesting and receiving a certificate of the CFO or an independent opinion as to the corporation's compliance with the applicable solvency, surplus, or other requirements for making a distribution.

2. Federal Securities Law Liability

Public company directors may also be personally liable under the federal securities laws—in some cases even when they act in good faith. In certain circumstances, negligence, by itself, is sufficient to establish liability. In other situations, liability may be imposed, subject only to due diligence or other defenses, without a finding of fault or intent to deceive. See Chapter 5 for a discussion of director duties under the federal securities laws.

3. Liability under Other Laws

Directors may be subject to personal liability under other state and federal statutes, such as antitrust, workplace safety, and environmental laws. Good faith and careful monitoring of management programs directed toward corporate legal compliance (including periodic briefings on the timely and proper functioning of compliance programs and any changes in them) and appropriately documenting such monitoring in minutes should provide substantial safeguards against any such personal liability.

B. PROTECTIONS

Several measures help to protect directors from personal liability: provisions in the articles or certificate of incorporation limiting liability, rights to indemnification, rights to advancement of legal expenses, and insurance. Of course, the best protection for directors is documented compliance with their duties.

1. Limitation of Liability

Most state corporation statutes permit a corporation's articles or certificate of incorporation to include a provision (commonly referred to as an "exculpation provision") eliminating or limiting the liability of directors (and, in some states, officers) to the corporation and its shareholders for monetary damages resulting from breaches of certain duties. These provisions most frequently eliminate exposure to claims by the corporation or by shareholders (either directly or derivatively on behalf of the corporation) for monetary damages for breaches of the duty of care under the law of the jurisdiction under which the corporation is formed. These provisions do not, however, cover claims for injunctive or other non-monetary relief or liabilities to third parties, and they do not protect a director from liabilities resulting from violations of federal law or laws of foreign nations or states other than the corporation's jurisdiction of incorporation. As a general rule, they do not protect directors from monetary liability for unlawful stock repurchases, dividends, or other distributions, actions or omissions in bad faith, breaches of the duty of loyalty, intentional violations of law, or actions when the director received an improper benefit.

2. Indemnification

Most state corporation statutes specify the circumstances in which the corporation is permitted to indemnify directors against liability and to reimburse or advance related reasonable expenses incurred in defending claims arising from their service as directors.

In general, directors must meet a certain standard of conduct before being indemnified. The standard for permissible indemnification in many state statutes is that the individual director must have acted in good faith and with a reasonable belief that the director's conduct was in (or not opposed to) the best interests of the corporation, and, in the case of a criminal proceeding, the director must also have had no reasonable cause to believe the conduct was unlawful. These statutes give corporations the power to indemnify directors in actions by third parties, including class actions, for expenses (including attorneys' fees), judgments, fines, and amounts paid in settlement. In some instances, however, indemnification is not permitted, even if the director has complied with applicable standards of conduct. For example, many jurisdictions prohibit indemnification for liability in derivative actions (i.e., actions brought by shareholders on behalf of the corporation), unless ordered by a court.

3. Advancement of Expenses

In addition to permitting indemnification, state corporation statutes generally permit a corporation to pay a director's legal expenses during the pendency of most lawsuits before final disposition of the proceeding. The cost of defending a claim (including an initial retainer) may be substantial, making advancement of expenses important. In most states, a director benefiting from such an advancement of expenses, however, must promise to repay the amount advanced if it is ultimately determined that the director is not entitled to indemnification.

4. Mandatory Indemnification and Advancement of Expenses

Many state statutes provide that indemnification for legal expenses is mandatory when (or to the extent that) the director is successful in defending a suit. In order to induce directors to serve, most corporations provide for mandatory indemnification and advancement of expenses under additional circumstances through provisions in their articles or certificate of incorporation, provisions in their bylaws, or through separate agreements with directors. In many instances, these provisions provide that directors are to be indemnified and advanced expenses to the fullest extent permitted by law. In other cases, director rights are more limited. Directors should understand the extent of their mandatory rights and any limitations on those rights.

5. Indemnification Agreements

Many corporations and their directors and officers enter into contracts to indemnify and advance expenses to them. These indemnification agreements perform three functions:

- they are enforceable against the corporation and, thus, give the indemnitee a right to sue the corporation for breach of contract, in addition to any other right the indemnitee may have under state law or a provision of the articles of incorporation, certificate of incorporation, or bylaws;
- they usually set forth various procedures for seeking and requiring the corporation to make indemnification and expense payments; and
- they often expand the scope of indemnification to the maximum extent permitted by applicable law, including so-called non-exclusivity provisions of some state corporation statutes that permit corporations to indemnify and advance expenses beyond the limits specifically required or permitted by statute.

It is generally thought that the extent of provisions expanding the scope of indemnification is limited by public policy, although there is no clear definition of what public policy would be in this regard.

6. Insurance

Most public and some (typically larger) private companies purchase directors and officers (D&O) liability insurance covering:

- the corporation for any payment of indemnification and advancements of expenses; and
- directors and officers, if the corporation is unwilling to pay indemnification or expense advancement obligations (perhaps because of a change in control) or is unable to pay such obligations (perhaps because of insolvency or because the claim is one for which indemnification or advancement is not permitted).

The relevant statutes in most jurisdictions permit the corporation to pay premiums for this insurance. Because directors and officers may not be able to access policies that also cover the corporation, corporations should consider purchasing policies that cover only non-management directors. Such policies often include terms more favorable to the insured (for example, no deductible) than policies that cover both the corporation and its directors.

Certain areas of activity, such as environmental, employee benefit, or antitrust matters, are often excluded from coverage under a typical D&O policy. Sexual misconduct-related claims may be excluded under some D&O policies, especially if they involve not only verbal but also physical harassment or assault. Coverage may also exclude conditions in existence at the time of the application for insurance. D&O insurance generally does not cover fraud, fines, insider trading, or criminal penalties, and it sometimes excludes punitive damages.

Insurance coverage is not available in every case. Most policies are written on a "claims made" (as compared to an "occurrence") basis, covering only defined claims lodged against directors during a specified period. In addition, the terms of coverage under differing policies are complex and may vary from insurer to insurer. Moreover, insurance markets change rapidly, and insurers may assert numerous reservations or defenses when claims are made. Therefore, directors are well advised to engage experts with knowledge and experience in reviewing D&O policies and current market conditions when renewing or reviewing D&O insurance coverage.

It is important for directors to understand the scope of the corporation's D&O insurance on a continuing basis, including the insuring clause, retentions/deductibles, limits, exclusions, and participating D&O carriers ("stacking" and reinsurance). Many boards require an annual presentation to directors on insurance coverage. Directors should ascertain the level of expertise of the person within the corporation responsible for negotiating the coverage or, in the alternative, determine whether an outside expert, familiar with current market conditions and policy and claim issues, is assisting in the process. Directors should also take care (as is true in the case of any insurance policy) in completing policy applications and questionnaires and inquire about the insurance carrier's reputation for handling insurance claims and its financial strength. These considerations may be as or more important than pricing. Disputes with the insurance carrier over coverage when litigation materializes are an unwanted and often costly distraction. D&O insurance is a complex area, and directors should seek assurance that the corporation's coverage does in fact afford the best protection practicably obtainable in the current marketplace. Finally, directors should inquire whether coverage extends to claims made beyond the directors' terms of service.